# Women Deans

## Patterns of Power

Carol Isaac

UNIVERSITY PRESS OF AMERICA,® INC.
*Lanham • Boulder • New York • Toronto • Plymouth, UK*

Copyright © 2007 by
University Press of America,® Inc.
4501 Forbes Boulevard
Suite 200
Lanham, Maryland 20706
UPA Acquisitions Department (301) 459-3366

Estover Road
Plymouth PL6 7PY
United Kingdom

Library of Congress Control Number: 2007923534
ISBN-13: 978-0-7618-3675-9 (paperback : alk. paper)
ISBN-10: 0-7618-3675-6 (paperback : alk. paper)

I dedicate this book to the memory of my sister,
Kathryn Isaac,
whose presence will always live in my soul.

# Contents

# Acknowledgments

I am very grateful to Dr. Linda Behar-Horenstein in the Department of Educational Policy and Administration, and to Dr. Mirka Koro-Ljungberg in the Department of Educational Psychology, my committee chairs and mentors at the University of Florida. Many other faculty, staff, and students from the College of Education have supported me during some very difficult times during the last four years; I thank you all. Finally, I would especially like to thank my partner, whose untiring patience, love, and humor have sustained me though some difficult times. Our partnership balances struggle and contentment, commitment and freedom, and has truly enlarged my life.

# Prologue: The Call

I remember the chill of hearing the message at 7:00 AM, Wednesday, "This is the Sunnyvale police department, please give us a call regarding your sister." The police had left a message at 9:00 PM on Tuesday the night before, but we had gone to bed early and hadn't heard it. Before calling, I went to take a shower. Somehow I wasn't ready to deal with whatever reality was coming. Perhaps I also knew intuitively that it was too late, because, by that time, it was. My sister had committed suicide Tuesday, May 27, 2003.

She was a clinical neurologist working at a well-known research institution and had spent the last several years attempting to obtain a tenured faculty position. This institution already had a history of not promoting women, and three women physicians had been forced to leave in the last several years. As with many prestigious institutions, faculty are recruited into tenured positions for research dollars. Often junior faculty place the work experience on their resume and go elsewhere for tenure. However, for a variety of reasons, my sister did not leave. . . . could not leave, and placed the entire blame on the institution for her act. The question whether an institution can be blamed for such a death can be debated, less debatable is the ominous effect of a female colleague killing themselves on other striving females in the profession. Intellectually I know that organizations do not kill people; those people make their own choices. Emotionally though, I knew my sister as a sensitive, bright, articulate person who cared about her patients and medical students.

I had had several conversations over the previous months with her about her job. Having been a reorganized healthcare manager myself, she had called me regarding conversations she had with her direct supervisor and department chair. She had been previously hired by an interim chair that had liked her work, but now had a new chair seeking to hire a tenured position to bring in research money; his goal was to replace her. I had recommended that she

take notes after each meeting with her supervisor. One document of her reflections read:

> He [supervisor] said building a national reputation in headache would be benefi-
> cial, but I have not done that yet. Would Dr. [chairman] be willing to give me a
> few years to do that, who knows? It is a clinical job and doesn't bring in money
> to the department like someone who brings in grants. I asked if my position was
> valued or needed. He said, of course, someone has to see the patients, but that
> could be anyone. He said even tenured faculty are not indispensable.

Under the best circumstances these meetings would have been horrible. Because my sister had been sleep-deprived for several years, her depression in
her pre-menopausal years deepened and made these events intolerable.

By noon on Wednesday, they had found her car at a roadside park with
cliffs that overlook the Pacific Ocean. My sister had loved the ocean. She
collected sea glass in Massachusetts where she had lived years before. She
had taken friends and family members over the Santa Monica Mountains on
Highway 17 to Santa Cruz many times. She loved the coastal mountain cliffs
of California; later I was told by friends that she would go there to "get away
from it all." In hindsight, this term provided new significance.

The police found her car Wednesday morning, and later found her body
crumpled at the base of a 275 foot cliff a quarter of a mile north of the park.
They called my mother, and she called me Wednesday night around 7:30; my
mother's words rang in my ears, "it's over." But it wasn't over; it had just be-
gun. My partner and I got to her house on Thursday night. It was chilling to
walk into that house as my sister had left it. Papers were strewn all over her
dining room table and clothes were everywhere in her bedroom, representing
to me the chaos of her mind during those last few hours. Two weeks prior,
my sister had received notification that her chair who had considered leav-
ing had decided to stay. My mother had just been out there the week before
responding to a call for help from my shaken sister. My mother reported that
the house had been clean when she got there, and my sister seemed settled
after her visit having found a new job and house.

Her reality was not clean and tidy as my mother had seen it. Suicide is a
"master of disguise" where truth remains hidden. My sister as a physician
knew that to tell anyone of her feelings could endanger her license to practice
medicine. My father had called her the day before her death and had reported
that her conversation was "scattered" with only superficial details; he said she
did not want to talk. I had talked to her two weeks prior to her death for fif-
teen minutes regarding her possible move to somewhere—she did not know
what to do. Later I realized that her panicked call was the date she had found
out her chair was staying, and that she would have to leave. I have replayed

that phone call and the sequence of events incessantly in my head, attempting to reconcile and justify my part in her death. I have not found an answer, but just more questions that dissolve into the insignificance of grief.

Amazing what little we present to the world, but especially to our families in times of crisis. I was in hyper-drive for months after her death with the soul purpose to take care of my sister in death as I had not been able to in life. I know now that I was endlessly attempting to restore a semblance of order to my family and my world within. That weekend, I boxed up valuables and mementoes to send to family while my partner sorted my sister's financial matters for the attorney. My mother was arriving on Monday night so we cleaned and picked up. I did not want my mother to see the house in such disarray. A sense of order to all this external chaos was necessary to help soothe my internal world. As we cleaned, we saw more evidence of my sister's inner turmoil. I needed to hide evidence of her insanity.

I was beginning a journey where a survivor's grief rambles to the next memory of their loved one and then the next. This grief has no structure, and feelings and thoughts meander without rhyme or reason. An uncovered memory begins a train of thought that constantly stops in the middle and reflects to another. C. S. Lewis described grief as a "long valley, a winding valley where any bend may reveal a totally new landscape" (1981, p. 69). A suicide survivors' grief is different in that while survivors' know "how" they died, we don't know "why," thus the endless search of their lives and our own—"what could I have done." In the months immediately following her death, family talk focused on memories of my sister and the "why" question; painful as some of it was. Perhaps my guilt was driving the compulsion to touch every part of my sister's life.

The first thing I did after entering her house the first night was to put her on robe to smell her presence. Her absence was unreal. As the week unfolded, I looked everywhere for signs of my sister. Strangely, there were two rental video tapes with a note to return them to such-and-such store. They were both light-hearted movies—not grim or dark. That first night I woke up at 3:00 AM and while my partner slept, I wandered the house aimlessly. Finally, there was stillness, and I wrote an epitaph as I sensed her presence, and felt complete- at least for a while. The epitaph reflected on her characteristics: her love for travel, her patients, her friends and family, her plants and animals. In the process of writing, I found empathy and compassion for my sister, and "was given a knowing that God loves the pained and afflicted even more." I had not set out to write my sister's eulogy, but it poured out of the stillness. I sensed how much pain my sister had been in, and I sensed that her pain was gone—the oppositional binary of hope and despair.

Other issues clamored for my attention. My sister's answering machine was filled with messages from worried co-workers and friends. I went to her church when we got back from the coast, and there was a need for a memorial service. One by one, I called her friends, shattering the silence and the hope that everything was all right. I went through her address book calling old friends that I knew and having them call others. The chain of life is long and a single event affects many. I realized that while my sister had been depressed for a long time, she was well-loved. Her friends told me stories, but mostly I listened to the shock of the news of her death in their voices. I heard the depth of remorse and concern. We were not the only ones who had lost; however, I felt strangely detached from them as if I was watching from a distance. I could not grieve with them fully. I was listening to them closely for fragments of my sister, and searching for parts of her in them. I perceived the intensity of their pain was directly proportional to the amount of love they had had for my sister.

Later in the week, we went to my sister's bank, met with the probate attorney, met with the minister about the funeral, and finally went to the medical school to clear out her office of her personal items. Of all the events of this week, this task was the most shocking for me. My mother, partner and I were met by two secretaries and led back to her office located behind the copy room. The office had not been touched and appeared to be waiting for my sister's return. I started to cry as we pulled down her diplomas and certificates, packed her curios, and loaded some of her books. The secretaries were very sympathetic, but we were surprised that none of her colleagues met us. The absence of their presence was deafening. As we left, my anger raged toward this institution that seemed to have so little regard for my sister's life. My sister's suicide note had said, "I'm so sorry to do this. But it's all become too much. I don't blame anyone except [institution]; they ripped up my life and made it impossible to cope."

In the context of her letter, her death, and the lack of personal interaction with her colleagues, my rage was probably understandable. Perhaps the staff sensed our anger and avoided us like the plague. In hindsight, I'm glad I did not meet her supervisor, as I probably would have behaved badly. Having been in management myself, I knew that the medical school was probably already circling the attorneys and had been told to avoid any hint of responsibility. Institutions serve and protect themselves. Institutions can act anonymously while individual interactions connect faces with actions; no wonder they did not want to meet us. Within a week, my sister's picture and vitae disappeared off the website of the medical school. In my mind, my sister's memory was being wiped away; suicide is unspoken, but resounds everywhere. Her absence was presence.

The chairman wrote a condolence letter to my mother after my sister's death that said:

I write to express my profound sadness at the passing of your daughter, Kathryn. She was an outstanding neurologist and teacher. I never met a physician who had more genuine concern for her patients and for their well being. This quality, and her superior attributes as a physician, earned her the respect of all of her colleagues and her students. (. . .) We honored Kathryn at our year-end party for the residents and faculty. I indicated that I hoped that Kathryn's legacy would be a renewed appreciation within the Department of the extremely important role that respect for colleagues and patients must play. Kathryn was our role model in this. . . .

When I compared this letter to the notes my sister had written about her meetings with her chair, I cannot begin to describe the feelings of confusion. What was reality? There are no words to describe my feelings regarding the disparity between my sister's perception of what was happening to her, and what the chairman wrote about her. Would Kathryn's death improve the atmosphere of respect in the medical school? Was my sister a martyr in her own right? We will never know. I do know of two women who left academia whom did not know my sister, but knew of her death. These women do not include several women physicians who were forced to leave this medical institution in recent years.

I could not return for her funeral the next Saturday, but recorded and transcribed the event so that other family members and friends could participate. As I listened to the tape, I was in awe of her contribution to the community and the medical school. I had never understood the depth of her commitment to her students and patients. One of her residents spoke of feeling inadequate and always being able to reach out to my sister who made him "feel incredibly loved." Another medical student knew my sister first as a patient and then as a student and reported how important she had been to the student community, and that she had "really touched so many students" at the medical school. One of her colleagues described her as a "real mensch," who not only referred patients to her, but also sought her immediately when he himself had a transient neurological episode. He described her as "very kind" and "humane." Here is an account of how one student perceived my sister:

I have known Dr. Isaac both as, I guess, a student at the medical school—she was my teacher for, I guess, four years ago. But I also got to know her as my doctor. I was diagnosed with cancer back in '99. I had it at two places, in my back, spinal cord cancer, and I had back pain for three months and then finally I went to see her. I had six to nine months left to live, most likely. I am—I wouldn't probably be here today if it wasn't for her. She ordered the MRI right there and then and I went through back surgeries and chemo and radiation for about a year and a half. And she continued to come in and see me in the hospital when I was going through my treatment. I saw her love as she would come and see me. I saw her caring and I am grateful to her for the impact she has had on my life and although she may not be with us today, physically, I feel that her soul has become part of my soul and I hope that in the people that I come in contact with, I continue to touch their lives through her love.

To be sure, these comments are in context of a memorial service; however, there is no better referral than for a colleague or student to choose someone they work with for their medical care. Her colleagues and students admired her but had no awareness of her depression and her difficulties at work. There were such different perceptions of her life between her friends and coworkers. I understand that there will always be things that are spoken and whispered. My mind floated between comments made at her funeral, to her notes from the meetings with her supervisor, to my mother's condolence letter from the chairman. Reality is not easily understood and is swayed by the context. I also have a "knowing" that my difficulty with comprehending the fragments of her last few days, were not unlike her search for a reality she could live with . . . or could not. No matter how others may have loved and admired her, she was isolated from that love, and that perception guided her final decision.

As the months passed, the "why" question perplexed me endlessly. My parents had undergone a tempestuous divorce when Kathryn was a senior in high school. Both my parents were physicians, and the conservative fifties gave way to the turbulent sixties with a new influx of feminism. I had always known that my father was conservative, and my physician mother was a strange mix of feminist and Republican, a product of her depression-era upbringing. I remembered my sister and father arguing politics, he on the right and she on the left. My sister seemed to become more conservative in her transition from being a sixties hippie to a physician, but not much.

I understood my sister's inner conflict as I looked at my own. I loved both my parents, but there was a drive to "win" that stemmed from their conflict. My personal history as my sister's, was fraught with attempts to gain approval of a male discourse; this drive to "win" back my father's attention (he had a new wife and family) never ceased and was largely unconscious. I gradually had a "knowing" of why she died; she could not tolerate being the "outcast" of another patriarchal discourse, even if it was an institution. Strangely enough, this "knowing" was confirmed by my sister's therapist who said that children routinely set up scenarios to resolve past traumatic events. I certainly had done this in personal and work-related relationships, but what makes some women "go off the cliff," and others persevere? There are other ways women abandon themselves: not engaging in their heart's desire, staying in abusive relationships, even ambushing their own success. I now sought some of these answers through my writing. For myself, this writing has become a "method of inquiry," "a way of 'knowing'-a method of discovery and analysis" (Richardson, 2000, p. 923). Here was a legitimate avenue to focus my energies and rejuvenate my soul. I was driven to understand how women negotiate power in academia.

# Chapter One

# Introduction

The authorial voice of leadership has been largely white male, and good practice has been considered to be the techniques and procedures of white male administrators (Grogan, 2003). Most gender research takes a binary approach that concentrates on the hierarchical patterns of power. Men and women use power consciously and unconsciously sustaining persistent and pervasive inequalities, and power is multidimensional. Historically, the written curricula and "null curriculum" send strong messages about what is important (Davidson, 1994, p. 335). There are rules within organizations concerning who can make statements and in what context. In educational administration, male voices have been the dominating and defining force.

In response, feminist theory is founded on the recognition of gender as a legitimate category of analysis (Scott, 1986). Feminist literature from the 1970s onwards is grounded in such disciplines as philosophy, sociology, psychology, and history that explored the significance of gender relations (Belenky, Clinchy, Goldberger, & Tarule, 1986). Flax (1990) argues that feminist theory aims "to analyze gender relations: how gender relations are constituted and experienced and how we think or, equally important, do not think about them" (p. 40). If we accept gender as a useful category of analysis to help us understand administration better, then we need to draw on the experiences of women in those positions. Biklen and Shakeshaft (1985) call for scholarship on women that focuses on how women perceive their own worlds. The belief is that this scholarship will contribute to a fuller comprehension of human behavior and society "since inadequate conception of the female experience distorts our perspectives on the human experience as a whole" (Grogan, 2003, p. 18).

Not only have women's authorial voices been diminished, but women's characteristics in leadership are indistinct. Most gender research takes a critical view from a binary "us" versus "them" approach with a strict focus on the hierarchical patterns of power. The usefulness of poststructuralism, a postmodern approach, is in its questioning and its insistence on understanding the relationship between knowledge and power. Power is multidimensional and once this is accepted, a more comprehensive understanding of the local context is achieved (Grogan, 2003). Qualitative research is not concerned with generalization, but emphasizes local context. Poststructuralism provides us with concepts that enable us to understand administration in terms shaded differently. This study's purpose is to examine patterns of discourse, subjectivity, resistance, and power and knowledge between women administrators in male versus female dominated fields using a feminist postructural lens and rhizoanalysis.

## RESEARCH QUESTIONS

In a qualitative study, the researcher seeks to discover, understand or describe. Qualitative research is used to best describe "how" something works rather than the quantitative perspective of "how well" something works (Borg, Gall & Gall, 1993). Qualitative research questions amplify the participants' cultures, relationships, qualities of practice, and beliefs. A feminist postructural approach explored these "women's arts of existence, or practices of the self, the things they do every day that make them who they are" (St. Pierre, 2005, p. 1). For this study, research questions include:

1. How do women leaders construct leadership and their identities within leadership discourse?
2. How do these women negotiate and produce power in higher education?

These questions form the basis of the research; however, they do not represent an exhaustive list.

## THEORETICAL FRAMEWORK

Although postmodernism and poststructuralism are terms often used interchangeably, postmodernism is more encompassing (Schwandt, 2001). To understand postmodernism, one must understand modernism. For modernist or positivist researchers, there is a "real" reality "out there" (Denzin & Lincoln,

2000, p. 176), and this reality is to be uncontaminated by human flaws. Modernism has great faith in the ability of reason to discover absolute forms of knowledge. However, postmodernism "refuses all semblance of the totalizing and essentialist orientations of modernist systems and thought. . . . Instead of representing clarity, wholeness, and continuity, postmodernism is committed to ambiguity, relativity, fragmentation, particularity, and discontinuity. . . . One is the antithesis of the other" (Crotty, 1998, p. 185). Adopting a postmodern theoretical position involves denying the existence of foundational knowledge on the grounds that no knowable social reality exists beyond the signs of language, image, and discourse" (Hargreaves, 1994, p. 39).

The methods and methodology of this research are embedded in the theoretical framework of poststructural feminism. Historically, feminist research has stemmed from the binary perspective of critical inquiry. Feminist theories arising from this body of literature differ from each other, but what loosely links them is their attention to "distinctively feminist issues [which are] the situation of women and the analysis of male domination" (Flax, 1990, p. 40). Although the critical perspective is a common way of viewing feminism, poststructural theory is another approach. Macey defines poststructuralism as a "reluctance to ground discourse in any theory of metaphysical origins, an insistence on the inevitable plurality and instability of meaning, a distrust of systematic scientificity, and the abandoning of the old enlightenment project" (2000, p. 309). Schwandt adds to this ambiguity by defining poststructuralism as the "decentering of the notion of the individual, self-aware condition of being a subject. . . . The 'I' is not immediately available to itself because it derives its identity only from its position in language or its involvement in various systems of signification" (2001, p.203). Schwandt also describes the theme of pantextualism where "everything is a text-and all text are interrelated . . ." (2001, p.203).

The theoretical framework of poststructuralism which emphasizes the instability of meaning and systematic methods lends itself to the use of the rhizome. The rhizome examines the contextual interactions of women in leadership through the unceasing "connections between semiotic chains, organizations of power, and circumstances relative to the arts, sciences, and social struggles" (Deleuze & Guattari, 1980/1987, p. 7). Rhizoanalysis, like searching for related topics on the internet, starts in one arena and travels to different plateaus within diverse layers of strata uncovering and discovering new vistas of knowledge.

As binaries were uncovered through the rhizome, they underwent deconstruction which "is a poststructural strategy for reading texts that unmasks the supposed 'truth' or meaning of text by undoing, reversing, and displacing taken-for-granted binary oppositions that structure texts (e.g., right over wrong, subject over object, reason over nature, men over women, speech over writing, and reality over appearance)" (Schwandt, 2001, p. 203-4). In place of an oppressive hierarchy, the emphasis is on the contextual interaction between individuals and institutions.

Feminist poststructural writings are built on critical feminist traditions that probe for research possibilities that "might, perhaps, not be so cruel to so many people" (St. Pierre & Pillow, 2000, p.1). Poststructuralism as a subset of postmodernism is linked to the work of the French writers, Foucault, Lyotard, Derrida, and Kristeva (Craib, 1992; Grogan, 2003; Sarup, 1988). The significant contribution of poststructuralism is that it enables us to understand administration in different terms from those that have been used in the past. These terms include discourse, subjectivity, power and knowledge, and resistance (Grogan, 2003).

## DEFINITION OF TERMS

Discourse is an intersubjective phenomenon, where discourse "is not a direct product of subjectivity and has a constituent role in the production of the symbolic systems that govern human existence" (Macey, 2000, p. 101). Foucault (1977/1980) uses the term 'discourse" to help us understand how we are positioned as subjects in different relationships with others. This understanding of the way we are positioned is dependent on our relative power in each discourse. Furthermore, these symbolic systems are ordered "through our linguistic description" (Mills, 2004, p. 47). How our text describes the world creates our discourse.

This evolving definition of discourse was influenced by Foucault's "discursive formation" which he described as "homogeneous fields of enunciative regularities" (Foucault, 1972/2002, p. 117). Discursive formation has also been defined as a "group of statements in which it is possible to find a pattern of regularity defined in terms of order, correlation, position and function" (Macey, 2000, p. 101). An example of discursive formation would be the variety of phenomena that include the roles men and women assume that produce the concepts of normalcy and deviation.

To understand subjectivity is to understand that discourses systematically form the objects of which they speak (Sarup, 1988, p. 70). Therefore, a man or woman who becomes an administrator is shaped or subjectified by that discourse. Subjectivity refers to "the conscious and unconscious thoughts and emotions of the individual, her sense of herself and her ways of understanding her relation to the world" (Weedon, 1997, p. 32).

For Foucault, "relations of force and power are involved at every level of a discursive formation; . . . because knowledge is always a form of power"

(Macey, 2000, p. 101). As Foucault suggests, there is an interdependence of power and knowledge; what counts as knowledge is the relative power of those who claim it; one hypothesis of power is that the "mechanisms of power are those of repression" (1977/1980, p. 91). There are rules within a discourse concerning who can make statements and in what context, and these rules "exclude some and include others" (Craib, 1992, p.186). In analyzing gender roles, "sexism comes to feel 'natural' or dominant within a culture, it does not allow us any real sense of how it would be possible to intervene and change that process" (Mills, 2004, p. 39).

However gender differences are understood, most feminist leadership analyses slips into an oppositional discourse between masculine and feminine leadership. In the construction of gendered leadership discourses, the literature presents masculine leadership as "competitive, hierarchical, rational, unemotional, analytic, strategic and controlling, and feminine leadership as cooperative, team working, intuitive/rational, focused on high performance, empathic and collaborative" (Court, 2005, p. 5). Leadership characteristics such as "aggression, vision, strength, determination, and courage are consistent with, and usually positively associated with the masculine traits that result from the ways boys are commonly socialized within American society" (Nidiffer, 2001, p. 103). Joseph Crowley (1994), in a historical study on college presidents, associated with leadership metaphors such as boss, superman, father, titan, hero, gladiator, and quarterback. In the discourse of educational administration, those with the power to define good practice are the male administrators whose experiences form the basis of most texts and much of the research of the profession.

The differences in discourse spark conflict. The "theoretical paradigm of difference is obsessed with the construction of identities rather than relations of power and domination, and concentrates on the effect of this difference . . ." (Gordon, 2001, p. 189). Education thus reproduces existing gender inequalities; however, feminist studies assert that all people have the capacity to resist oppression (Weiler, 2003). If the definition of knowledge is expanded to include others' voices, then it is to be expected that such new knowledge will include a resistance to the formerly accepted knowledge claim (Grogan, 2003). Foucault thought that although the subject is affected by knowledge and power, it is "irreducible to these," so the "subject actually functions as a pocket of resistance to established forms of power/knowledge, in the present age" (Alvesson & Skoldberg, 2001, p. 230). These insights ". . . warn us to expect conflict, and, secondly allow us to question taken-for-granted assumptions, particularly about the implications of local policies and practices" (Grogan, 2003, p.20).

In applying the postmodern concepts of discourse, subjectivity, power and knowledge, and resistance to women administrators, we can see how these concepts can expand and contribute to the educational leadership field. Administrators have been encouraged to think and behave in ways that have been dictated by a white, male-dominated discourse shaped by a different age. This phenomenon is very similar to the example that Foucault gives where "TV and cinema act as an effective means . . . of reprogramming popular memory in which people are shown not what they were but what they must remember having been" (Woods, 1999, p. 197). Women administrators are so few that their presence remains the exception, not the rule. Certainly, their practices have rarely had a voice in administration research because they have been excised (Behar & Gordon, 1995).

## SUBJECTIVITY STATEMENT

I grew up as a child of the sixties, the daughter of two physicians. I had been a proponent of the feminist movement for years until I joined a fundamentalist movement during my twenties. In my thirties, my life experiences led me to reject "binary" thinking to espouse more moderate reactions. In graduate school, I became fascinated with the critical works of Freire, and those of the poststructuralist, Foucault. Culture is linked with the shaping of social groups creating a theoretical paradox and implying opposition between culture and society. In previous research while interviewing faculty, I had noticed difficulty distancing myself from the content of the interviews due to my previous experience in management, my interest in future employment, and especially my interest in power structures. During this study I journaled my thoughts to help clarify my researcher bias and delineate my ideas for peer debriefing and external audits.

As a previous corporate manager in a large healthcare organization, I saw how a new CEO can dramatically shift the culture of an organization. Like healthcare, education faces a budget crisis and the neoliberal philosophy of efficiency, accountability, and measurement of outcomes, the watchwords of cultural change in education. With this neoliberal influence comes a hierarchical system that intensifies competition and a patriarchal discourse. The hospital administration brought in a consultant for a series of presentations emphasizing an organizational focus of transitioning employees (including managers) and cost-cutting, rather than building long-term organizational loyalty. This ideology was in sharp contrast to my values of loyalty and commitment. I slowly changed my management style over the years from a patient/employee service focus to a cost-cutting focus with disastrous long-term results. In the short-term, I received praise from administration as I slashed my expenses by improving efficiency and productivity; however, years later under different management, employee retention still suffered. Under the leadership of the CEO over a five year period, only three managers out of nearly fifty remained; although the hospital has continued to earn national recognition.

So, how could I have "sold out" not only others, but even more importantly, myself? Expectations were high and consequences were apparent with the number of managers that had been "reorganized" out of the organization. The institutional discourse shaped my behavior, and my role with employees became increasingly binary- "us" versus "them." My managerial experience gives me a unique perspective of leadership as higher education transitions into a corporate model. Although women leaders are seen to promote cooperation and collaboration in organizations in contrast to competitive and hierarchical systems, this poststructural study sought new patterns of discourse, resistance, subjectivity, power and knowledge in higher education administration.

## SIGNIFICANCE

The contribution of poststructuralist theoretical perspective is in its questioning and its insistence on understanding the relationship between knowledge and power. A feminist poststructuralist examines leadership in terms of "discourse, subjectivity, power and knowledge, and resistance" (Grogan, 2003, p. 18). Also, people undergo particular conflict and fragmentation if the discourses within which they are immersed are not aligned with each other. For example, a woman administrator may experience tension and stress as she tries to reconcile the discourse of educational administration with that of mothering because the two make different demands on her (Grogan, 2003). This study attempted to ascertain patterns of power and difference of these women leaders.

## LIMITATIONS

Besides the inherent limitations of limited sample sizes and generalizations that stem from using a qualitative research design, there are other limitations from a poststructural perspective. One problem associated with poststructuralism involves a complicated view of power because its nature can be detrimental to the social politics of resistance. This view of politics is not "oppositional in contesting the mainstream . . ." (St. Pierre & Pillow, 2000, p. 67). Poststructuralists do not focus on a simple hierarchical view of men oppressing women, but a view of systematic genderized discourses where even "identity dissolves in a sea of meaningless differences, nothing stable and secure will remain upon which a politics of resistance can be built" (St. Pierre & Pillow, 2000, p. 64). Waugh stated that, "feminism cannot sustain itself as an emancipatory movement unless it acknowledges its foundation in the discourses of modernity" (Crotty, 1998, p. 195). Feminism as a political movement is dependent on a critical binary state of "us" and "them," and historically, feminist research has stemmed from the binary perspective of critical inquiry. However, poststructuralism examines and exalts difference rather than oppression between individuals and institutions.

Another difficulty with poststructuralism is the implicit epistemological stance of subjectivism. In subjectivism, "meaning does not come out of an interplay between subject and object but is imposed on the object by the subject" (Crotty, 1998, p. 9). The reader of the text is the creator of meaning (Crotty, 1998); thus, people form their own interpretation of the text based on their own experiences, perceptions, and expectations. As a researcher, my interpretation of the data was diffused through the lenses of my subjectivity making even general conclusions and implications difficult. What grounds the results is the support of the literature, and an incessant adherence to the theoretical perspective. Before data analysis, I would spend hours immersing myself in deconstructive thought and then clarify my bias with peer review and debriefing. During my analysis, these practices averted my initial impressions to simply conform my data to categories and cultivated the deconstructive complexity through repeated failure. This "practice of failure" transformed, my "impossibility into possibility where a failed account occasions new kinds of positioning" (Lather, 1996, p. 3). These "failures" stimulated me to always look outside my own discourse. In this way my practices confronted the dangerous illusion of conventional scientific method that concludes that the world is much simpler than it truly is, thus enlarging the textual representation (Denzin & Lincoln, 2000).

While not all anticipated criticism can be considered, another limitation of this study lies in the lack of direct comparison of these women's voices to men in leadership positions. Men were not interviewed because of the preponderance of men's views in the leadership discourse. While interviews with male deans might have widened the results, the emphasis of this research was on women's representation of leadership in higher education. Adding male participants would have promoted further delineation between genders thus lessening the benefits of a feminist postructural perspective which encourages the avoidance of absolutes and expanding current reality.

*Chapter Two*

# Strata of Knowledge

## INTRODUCTION

This chapter connects previous research concerning the aspects of women's identity as leaders, definitions of leadership, descriptions of power, and how women negotiate power. The term "feminism" has many layers of meaning that has been deepened by Julia Kristeva, a poststructuralist with a feminist focus. Much research has been done on women in academia; however, much less has been written on women leaders in higher education with the exceptions of some historical writings about the first women deans. Adding to this history were family memoirs about my great aunt who was the first women dean at a small Mennonite college. This story represents the first layer of stratum in this rhizome.

## PREDECESSORS—MY GREAT AUNT HELEN

After my sister's death, I longed to know those she had loved. When Kathryn would visit our hometown, she would always go visit our Great Aunt Helen. Since I was seven years younger, I never really understood her attraction to an older widow who lived in an old clapboard house next to the campus of Bethel, the local Mennonite college. She was born in 1890 and died in 1981, but her son was still alive and had some archives from her life. I interviewed him and transcribed the text. In this interaction, I came to understand parts of my legacy from a female predecessor. I had received an inheritance from a female kin who left signs of "strength, autonomy, or courage that [women] will need in daring to aspire to a literary vocation" (O'brien, 1987, p. 16).

9

Although she was a faithful Mennonite who stopped working as soon as she married, my Great Aunt Helen gave those who knew her a familial resource for the social construction of gender. Aunt Helen was the first women to graduate from Bethel College in 1912, and later became Dean of Women until she married in 1920. She had taught at the high school academy, and taught German and "Elocution and Physical Culture" to women college students during her years as dean. Aunt Helen was a charter member of the Women's International League for Peace and Freedom and corresponded with Jane Addams in Chicago, the prominent social reformer. As a Mennonite, she held to a pacifist position, and was very active in the league on a local level. Aunt Helen was also involved in The Institute for International Relations, a movement for peace, which brought Martin Luther King to speak at Bethel in 1961.

Besides having a "practical Christian faith" which promoted pacifism, she inherited an "intellectual curiosity" from her father Jacob. Great Aunt Helen had grown up in the same house with her two aunts, Susan and Elizabeth Isaac, who were the first women doctors in the state of Kansas during the late nineteenth and early twentieth centuries. My father's memoirs tell of how his father, Arnold Isaac, became a doctor because he wanted to be able to own a car to make house calls (a 1912 Buick) like his aunts. Therefore, my great, great aunts were the beginning of a long line of physicians.

Aunt Helen was known to provide "thoughtful and attentive listening and counseling," especially to new women coming to Bethel. Her son reminisced how she had "this easy, natural way of talking." Her son described her as a "constant presence in the college community" who was involved in campus activities for seventy years. He also described her as having "devout, basic Christian convictions," "a tolerant spirit" and as an individual who "was not rigid." Aunt Helen spoke eloquently and considerately of others and was remembered as having "a forgiving spirit and faith in the essential goodness of persons even when they disappointed her." No wonder my sister liked visiting her.


## DEANS OF WOMEN

The image of prudish, dowdy house mothers often comes to mind when envisioning the women deans of the past. Initially Oberlin and Antioch colleges had boarding houses for women students in the mid-1900s to protect women from the terrible "dangers" of male students with a female supervisor (Nidiffer & Bashaw, 2001, p. 136). Charles Finney, president of Oberlin, recommended to the University of Michigan that they hire a "wise and pious matron" to supervise women students before adding co-education (Holmes,

1939, p. 109). The pattern of hiring "deans of women" began in the 1890s in Midwestern co-educational colleges to chaperone the influx of women students. This position played a historical role by being "the first systemic, administrative response in higher education to cope with a new, and essentially unwelcome, population" (Nidiffer & Bashaw, p. 136). This began the trend in higher education of hiring administrators for new marginalized populations.

The co-education cause was taken up by educational reformers who wanted teachers, a largely female occupation. However, the campus environment was at times openly hostile; therefore administrators sought deans of women. William Rainey Harper's desire to make the University of Chicago into a western Yale prompted him to hire Alice Freeman Palmer, the former president of Wellesley College, as a history professor and dean of women (Nidiffer & Bashaw, 2001). Palmer added Marion Talbot as her assistant and in 1895 Talbot became dean when Palmer retired. Talbot was instrumental in creating the National Association of Deans of Women (NADW) in 1916, which transformed the housemother role into a profession. These women who were hired to conduct bed checks and chaperone actually were early advocates for females, representing well-educated, well-qualified, and intelligent women who could "exercise administrative skills and professional leadership" (Treichler, 1985, p. 24). Deans of women not only provided leadership to help female students cope with the hostile climate of the co-educational environment, but also acquired much needed housing. Families were reluctant to send their daughters to campuses that provided no housing and so boarding houses were used. As the numbers of female students increased, women deans were able to procure dormitories and scholarship halls for students. As female students became commonplace on Midwest campuses, higher education provided opportunities where educated women could find administrative positions; however, "some deans of women positions were analogous to home economics departments for academics" where it "became a female ghetto of sorts with the inevitable glass ceiling" (Nidiffer, 2000, p.4).

The most influential women contributing to the evolution of the profession were: "Marion Talbot, University of Chicago, 1892-1925; Mary Bidwell Breed, Indiana University, 1901-6; Ada Comstock, University of Minnesota, 1906-12; and Lois Mathews, University of Wisconsin, 1911-18" (Nidiffer & Bashaw, 2001, p. 139). Talbot founded the Association of Collegiate Alumnae (ACA), the predecessor of the American Association of University Women (AAUW), and was the main proponent of the professionalization of women deans. Breed's entrance to Indiana University met resentment from male faculty and students, and even from women students who thought they did not need disciplining. Breed reversed these sentiments through collaboration and self-government in an era that did not recognize women's contributions to leadership.

Ada Comstock helped women deans develop expertise and a scientific approach by articulating needs and initiatives. Comstock was dedicated to providing women a "sense of community, leadership roles, employment and intellectual opportunities" (Nidiffer & Bashaw, 2001, p. 146). She devoted much energy in finding gainful employment and developing career aspirations for women students. Lois Matthews, who was the first woman to pass Harvard's Ph.D. examination in history, sought equal status for women deans as members of the faculty. She negotiated her title as dean and the rank of associate professor at Wisconsin. Matthews, who published articles and a book on New England, brought the deanship to the same intellectual height as her academic career. All these women transformed the deanship from the role of house-mother into a profession that eventually became student affairs.

## WOMEN IN ACADEMIA

There is an abundance of feminist scholarly writings with a critical binary emphasis with themes of subservience and silence. Joan Acker's (1990) theory of "gendered organizations" recognized that organizational hierarchies are not gender neutral. Park (1996) described a gendered division of labor where sex-neutral corporations and bureaucracies are dominated by masculine structures that lead to advantages for males and disadvantages for female employees. These concepts reflect Foucault's "technologies of the self," (1988) which are concrete, socially and historically located institutional practices which construct our sense of who we are. Higher education is constituted of patriarchal hierarchies where women's status is considered marginalized and equated with lesser competence and credibility; women perceive difficulty obtaining research funds, conducting collaborative research with men, having their scholarly work seen as inferior and devalued, and being rated more negatively by students than men on student evaluations (Carroll, Ellis, & McCrea, 1991).

Acker and Feuerverger suggest that it is "what the university stands for, and what it rewards and what it ignores, that is at issue" (1996, p. 417). Women perceive a gendered reward structure where research and administration are seen as masculine, highly compensated skills, and teaching as an "emotional labor" that is considered feminine and non-essential (Bellas, 1999). Park stated that "research separates the men from the boys . . . and the women" (1996, p. 50). In 1990, one study found that 43% of male faculty, but only 36% of female faculty taught 8 or less hours a week, while 11% of female and 8% of male faculty spent greater than 17 hours per week teaching (Park, 1996). Toutkoushian (1999) found that women spend more time teaching and less doing research. Differences in research productivity are explained by women's structural position in departments where they carry heavier teaching loads, bear greater responsibility for undergraduate education, have more service commitments, and less access to graduate teaching assistants, as well as travel funds, research monies, and equipment. Women spend more time on pedagogical efforts than men, creating collaborative learning opportunities for students.

Promotion and tenure create considerable stress for women, although they often publish more than their male counterparts to ensure promotion. They produce lower levels of research output than men, but no difference was noted in the number of citations received per article; less research output does not mean lower quality (Toutkoushian, 1999). Women are less likely than men to be found among tenured faculty/ full professors because they progress at slower rates than men. While doctoral degrees granted to women have increased from 14% in 1970 to 39% in 1995, they earn lower shares of doctorates in engineering, mathematics, physical sciences, and business. Women obtained 21% of educational doctorates in 1970 and 62% in 1995; women composed 33% of faculty at all institutions in 1992, but 45% of part-time faculty (Toutkoushian, 1999).

Jean Baker Miller coined a phrase, "doing good and feeling bad" to describe women's experience in academia (Acker & Feuerverger, 1996, p. 401). Acker and Feuerverger interviewed 27 full and associate professors to gain an understanding of women who had at least one promotion in higher education. These transcripts, full of disillusionment, described women as working excessively hard, taking responsibility for supporting others (colleagues and students), being "good department citizens," and "feeling bad" (p. 408). These women perceived an unequal division of labor with women working harder, and an expectation that women will take greater responsibility for the nurturing and housekeeping side of academic life. They described a gendered division of labor where "the fact that women have been seen as 'naturally' suited to [teaching] has served to disguise its potential for exploitation and to discourage women from expressing 'outlaw emotions' such as envy and resentment that might be at odds with the caring script" (p. 402). This gendered division of labor assumes that women will have primary responsibility for nurturing the young and serving men, but "receive little credit for doing so" (p. 403). These women "sense that the academic reward system is out of sync with their preferences, that they are working harder than they should and that they have a disproportionate share of responsibilities for the mundane service side of university work and for the emotional well-beings of the students" (p. 404). The repetitive themes of inequality of workload, the expectation of caring for others, being "good department citizens" and not feeling "good enough" in a reward system of constant assessment are considered part of housewife roles, similar to those found in the historical discourse. Women have to be nurturing or be considered failures or perfectionists and face "chilly climate stories" (p. 409). Men are not faced with the same expectations.

Women, discouraged from pursuing their scholarly interests and workload, wish to speak for women's equity in acts of resistance; however, outspoken women concerned about the needs of female students will jeopardize their positions at the university. They are expected to advocate for women's issues, but this places them in a position of vulnerability where they may find themselves ridiculed, ignored, and disrespected (Carroll, Ellis & McCrea, 1991). Afraid of being perceived as "bitchy" and a target of gossip and ridicule, these women find little other recourse but silence.

In response to internalized sexist messages, women tend to silence themselves and accommodate others, rather than asserting their own opinions and feelings; however, much of the burden for creating change has rested on the women faculty themselves (Bronstein & Farnsworth, 1998). Those female professors who achieved success sometimes distance themselves as a "queen bee," or in the best scenario, transition into a women's advocate (Lincoln, 1986, p. 116).

Inappropriate sexual attention was reported significantly more often by women than by men regardless of their length of time at the university. Women experienced direct incidents of "harassing and discriminatory behaviors in their day-to-day interactions more than did men" (Bronstein & Farnsworth, 1998, p. 565). Sexual harassment is defined as "verbal or physical conduct of a sexual nature, imposed on the basis of sex . . . that denies, limits or provides different . . . treatment" (Paludi & Barickman, 1991, in Dey, Korn, & Sax, 1996, p. 151). In regards to academic rank, professors and assistant professors reported harassment at a rate of one-half to one-third of that reported by full professors. The study speculated that these results might have occurred because these professors had longer employment at the institutions; however, they concluded that sexual harassment has many inherent complexities with the "interplay between the concepts of position power" (p. 169). Another explanation to consider is that as women ascend the ranks of status, they become a greater challenge to the men around them and a target for interplays of power.

## WOMEN IN HIGHER EDUCATION ADMINISTRATION

Women in higher education administration have achieved a greater height of status and prestige. However, Sandler reported that female administrators "remain concentrated in a small number of low-status areas that are traditionally viewed as women's fields (nursing, home economics, education), or in care-taking roles (student affairs), or in other academic support roles" (Park, 1996, p. 54). More women aspired to lower-level administrative positions than men. Aspirations became nearly equal when considering the position of university vice president, but few females aimed for the position of university president. Many women wanted to serve as chair, or director/coordinator of departments.

This research seems to show that females perceive a "glass ceiling," sensing obstacles that did not affect men in their climb up the career ladder; females reported homemaking and child care as the toughest social barriers to advancement (Shultz & Easter, 1997). Other institutional barriers included: heavy workloads, bureaucracy, higher education requirements and lack of funds to meet them, committee demands, limited tenure tracks, research/ publication demands, and the "good old boys" network. In this same study not one male out of 93 men cited family responsibilities as a barrier to career advancement.

Very few males or females regarded opportunities for males and females as equal. Marshall and Jones (1990) found no statistically significant relationship between women's salaries, childbearing and administrative levels in higher education; however, qualitative responses from 147 participants had 63% reporting that childbearing had a negative effect while only 30% reported a positive effect. Although women reported that the satisfaction of family life outweighs career difficulties, these same women administrators reported paying a high personal price in maintaining of their careers (Marshall & Jones, 1990).

With regard to women in primarily male-dominated fields, women have historically always played a subservient role, especially in medical fields as nurses and technicians taking orders from the "male" physician. In 1949, women comprised 12% of post-war medical school graduates, and by the mid-fifties this number dropped to 5%; this was even lower than in 1941 (Solomon, 1985). In 1960, 758 women represented 5% of medical students (Martin et al., 1988). This number has gradually increased since that time to 49.6% in 2005, and while these percentages give the appearance of a positive trend, in 2005 women represented 15% of all full professors teaching clinical medicine (AAMC Data Book, 2005). Increased graduation rates have not reduced the prevalence of sexism, and 47% of women physicians have experienced gender-based harassment (harassment related to being female in a male environment), and 37% reported sexual harassment that included a physical component (Frank et al., 1998). In her book, *Walking Out on the Boys*, Frances Conley, a Stanford neurosurgeon, wrote that "medical school is and remains an institution of rigid hierarchies--almost an archetypal patriarchal society" (1998, pg. 4). The everyday world of physicians is shaped around a "rigid hierarchy of authority and power," and "learn to normalize their experiences of mistreatment and abuse" (Hinze, 2004, p. 103).

Higher education's statistics are only slightly better. In the early forties, women represented 27.7% of all academic personnel. This number fell to 24.5% in 1950 then to 22% in 1960. Women earning Ph.D.s dropped to 10-12% in the 1950's from 16-18% in the 1930's (Solomon, 1985). Historically, males have predominately comprised most of higher education faculty. From 1925 to 2000, the percentage of female full-time faculty has increased from 19% to 24%; in 1989, 22% of tenured faculty were female, and in 1998, the number increased to 26% (Wenniger & Conroy, 2001). While women hold 39% of all faculty positions, these positions are primarily adjunct and part-time. With educational cutbacks, fewer tenure-track positions, and more restrictive criteria for tenure, there is a new class of "gypsy scholars, an intellectual "proletariat" who are predominately female (Park, 1996, p. 50).

In salaries, women faculty are paid 77% of what their male counterparts earn, just a little more than the two-thirds level at which women were paid in the fifties. Part of this difference is women being concentrated in the lower-paying fields such as nursing and education. Gender has a "statistically significant direct, indirect, and total effect on salary attainment, with men academics having higher earnings than women colleagues when controlling for other variables" (Smart, 1991, p. 520). In 1969 men in academia earned 30% more than women, in 1984 men earned 23% more, and in 1991 women earned 7% less (Toutkoushian, 1999). These studies among many others indicate that higher education discriminates against women (Wenniger & Conroy, 2001). Some have argued that women expect too much and should be socialized to cope with the situation as it is. In reality, women accommodate to academia discourse; they are shaped by and assimilate into its culture.

## LEADERSHIP

Deconstructing the term "leadership" requires understanding its definition and how it's used. In this section, an overview of the various characteristics of leadership will be outlined with its associated skills, attitudes, and behaviors. "Leadership" is a term that everyone seems to understand, but have difficulty in defining (Perino & Perino, 1988). The terms "leadership" and the closely related term "management" are embedded within a masculine discursive voice. Leadership has broader implications than management and includes the achievement of organizational goals. Hershey, Blanchard, and Johnson define leadership as whenever one person attempts to influence the behavior of an individual or group regardless of reason (2001, p. 9). Warren Bennis, a leadership scholar, differentiated between management and leadership:

> Leaders conquer the context-the volatile, turbulent, ambiguous surroundings that sometimes seem to conspire against us and will surely suffocate us if we let them-while managers surrender to it. The manager administrates; the leader innovates. [ ] The manager has his eye on the bottom line; the leader has his eye on the horizon. The manager imitates; the leader originates. The manager accepts the status quo; the leader challenges it. . . . Managers do things right; leaders do the right things. (cited in Carter-Scott, 1994, p. 12)

Embedded phrases used such as "challenge," "conquer the context," "eye on the bottom line" or "horizon," and "do the right things," not only distinguish between the terms "leadership" and "management," but portray a pragmatic, hierarchical discourse. This ideology echoes the scientific management approach of Fredrick Taylor, emphasizing production and efficiency.

Several authors identify and define characteristics of good leaders. Passow (1988) viewed leadership as a group interaction with situational goals and with the ability to help others achieve goals. Sergiovanni (1990) identified four styles of leadership: bargaining, building, bonding, and banking. He defines a successful leader as one who strives to become a leader of leaders, has the ability to create other leaders, and embodies a commitment to ideas, values, and beliefs instead of power and control; these characteristics allow for a moral rather than institutional or psychological authority (Sergiovanni, 1990). Karnes and Chauvin (2005) proposed that leaders should possess a fundamental understanding of leadership as well as skills for speech, written communication, character-building, decision-making, problem-solving, personal, group dynamics, and planning. These authors also believe that these skills are teachable and are assessed through their leadership training programs.

Porter (1989) viewed the promotion of "ownership" by leaders created effective empowerment. These leaders must listen and recognize the value in others, create opportunities for progressive roles for others, reward competency, negotiate barriers, promote collegial interaction, and create teams for organizational problem solving, and help individuals understand how their roles contribute to the collective whole. All these behaviors are to be done without managing and controlling.

"Power," an important structure in leadership discourse, is defined as "influence potential," where different types of power are emphasized to "maximize effectiveness" (Hershey, Blanchard, & Johnson, 2001, p. 204). Leaders use power to create change. These authors distinguish between different types of power using language such as "coercive," "connective," "reward," "legitimate," "referent," "informative," and "expert" power (p. 213). Power is defined and identified, but also segmented into strata for a hierarchical leadership discourse.

How men and women enact power illustrates the oppositional discourse between masculine and feminine leadership. In a 1998 study, Brunner and Schumaker found that male superintendents tended to use power to achieve their own view of a community's common good rather than using their position to pursue the collective common good. The "power-over" concept was thought to be a masculine concept of power; although Brunner reported that the power-over is not the concept of power that every man holds. There has been less research on the "power-with" concept of power which is considered a feminine model. While not exclusively feminine, this concept of power is illustrated in topics such as collaborative decision-making, site-based management, and authentic participation where power is collective (Kanter, 1977, 1979; Harstock, 1987; Habermas, 1986; Wartenberg, 1990; Isaac, 1993; Miller, 1993). Hannah Arendt (1972) described collaborative power as a method to establish relationships among people to solve difficult social conditions. Miller (1993) suggested that women's identities demand that power is used to benefit the broader community and not used selfishly or destructively. In a study of women in state legislatures, Kirkpatrick (1974) found women searched for solutions to serve the common good where men competed to advance their own interests.

The "power-over" and "power-with" concepts of power are reminiscent of Jane Roland Martin's (1985) description of the productive/reproductive dichotomy of societal processes. Martin believed that these societal processes are gender related as well as the traits our culture associates with them. According to American stereotypes, men are "objective, analytical, rational, interested in ideas and things; they have no interpersonal orientation; they are not nurturant or supportive, empathic or sensitive" (Martin, 1985, p. 193). The productive processes include political, cultural and economic tasks and functions, where the reproductive processes include caring for the family helping the sick, and running the household. Kirkpatrick's finding that women leaders are motivated to serve the common good is a genderization that extols the feminine virtues of nurturance and care. These virtues have historically motivated women to create solutions for societal problems and thus aspire to leadership. The authorial voice and practice of white male administrators has created a productive discourse relegating the reproductive processes of service and nurturing to the "ontological basement" (Martin, 1985, p. 15).

Metaphors are used as a "device of the poetic imagination and the rhetorical flourish-a matter of extraordinary rather than ordinary language" (Lakoff & Johnson, 1980, p. 3). The metaphor represents the everyday functioning and defines perceptual realities. Metaphorical language is an important source of evidence of what is the lived experience of people. To understand subjectivity is to understand that discourses systematically form the objects of which they speak (Sarup, 1988, p. 70). Therefore, a man or woman who becomes an administrator is shaped or subjectified by that discourse. Subjectivity refers to the "conscious and unconscious thoughts and emotions of the individual, her sense of herself and her ways of understanding her relation to the world" (Weedon, 1997, p. 32). Because poststructuralism suggests that discourse forms the objects of which they speak, it was important to examine the speech patterns of these women leaders.

Examining the extensive literature on "leadership" provides a metaphorical window into the authorial voice. Typical leadership book titles include: *Leading with Soul, Leadership on the Line, Managing by Values, and Dare to Lead.* When the reader opens the cover of these books, the table of contents reveals sensationalized phrases as its own discursive practice. A table of contents of a typical book, *100 Ways to Motivate Others,* uses phrases such as "creating a dynamic work place," "coach the outcome," "be the cause not the effect," "accelerate change," "score the performance," "lead from the front," "use your best time for your biggest challenge," "coach your people to complete," "make it happen today," "pump up your e-mails," "deliver the reward," and "decide to be great" (Chandler & Richardson, 2005). This language is used to develop leadership skills and to motivate people, suggesting that all people can become leaders (Passow, 1988). These embedded symbols portray a masculine, hierarchical discourse.

These authors emphasize the "game" aspect of leadership. Winning is what's important to the players and supercedes the feminine collaboration and cooperation. Leadership is typically a vertical process, a top-down mentality where a horizontal approach to leadership builds teamwork and unity in an organization. The intersection between the vertical and horizontal define the leadership style within the organization. A horizontal leadership promotes collaboration and empowerment of followers, but can slow the decision-making process. Academia historically has been an institution where professors with tenure have the power of job security. These academic elites have been very vocal in their demands of leadership without direct impunity. However, greater accountability creates pressure within institutions to perform, and faculty sense with disillusionment the vertical movement of power associated with a loss of decision-making and ownership of the goals of the institution.

Academic leaders have greater pressure to conserve resources and manage personnel more effectively than ever before. Since the Eighties, the changing culture of neoliberalism means "fewer workers must produce more for less; globalization is widely invoked as the inexorable force that makes this imperative rational" (Peters, 2001, p.316). This umbrella of neo-liberalism sees corporate and government involvement as replacing "privacy and freedom from interference with passivity, dependence, the colonization of individual wills," and advocates "policies promoting privatization, consumer sovereignty, user-pays, self-reliance, and individual enterprise, as the solution to all economic and social ills" (p.125). For many workers the result is white and blue collar jobs that are benefit-free, temporary, and easily replaceable; far fewer jobs are permanent, fulltime positions.

Higher education is not exempt from these trends. The Organization for Economic Cooperation and Development's (OECD) publication, *Universities Under Scrutiny,* recommended that existing institutions "adapt: more career-oriented courses; greater emphasis on applied research and development; planning for technology transfer and knowledge diffusion; greater accountability and responsiveness of institutions; increased productivity and efficiency" (1987, p.3). Henry Giroux (2001) describes the new hidden curriculum of higher education as the "creeping vocationalization and subordination of learning to the dictates of the market" (p.34). In this climate of accountability, performance becomes a kind of ontology in the "discourse of quality" (Luke, 2001, p. 62). Lyotard (1979/1984) called this institutional representation "performativity." Administration and faculty are being driven to greater accountability and efficiency as never before.

## THE BINARY OF FEMINISM

Feminism means "essentially that a women's or gender perspective is applied to a variety of social phenomena" (Alvesson & Skoldberg, 2001, p. 209). There have been multiple brands of feminism, ranging from liberal feminism that primarily seeks sex equality to radical feminism that "distances itself from the male-dominated society in its entirety" (p. 209). Male-dominated society is characterized by "individualism, hierarchy, lack of feeling, impersonality, the competitive mentality, etc" (p. 212). The thesis that supports this brand of feminism is that the relationship between the sexes is one of "inequality and oppression" (Macey, 2000, p. 123).

The term "feminism" was first used in the 1830's. Socialist Charles Fourier stated that, "the degree of women's emancipation was the measure of the emancipation of society as a whole" (Macey, 2000, p. 123). The term became more widely used in the 1890's during the suffragette movement in Britain and the United States. Most historians would agree that modern feminism emerged from the French and American revolutions. In France, Olympe de Gouges published *Declaration of the rights of women and of the female citi-*

*zen,* and in England, Mary Wollstonecraft published *The Vindication of the Rights of Woman.* The campaign to obtain the vote was considered the first wave of feminism, and the second was the women's liberation movement of the 1970's, with Simone de Beauvoir and Betty Friedan representing the catalysts. Since the 1980's, there has been a backlash of criticism against feminism fought largely by the media which stated feminism had "gone too far" (Macey, p. 124). However, in the nineties, a new generation of feminists contended that women must abandon the old "victim feminism" in favor of "power feminism" (p. 124), which promotes economic equality with men, and a focus on liberation for both genders.

## SOCIAL FEMINISM: VICTIMIZATION & POWER

The second wave of feminism emphasized the gender differences in power. Feminist reproduction theorists share a belief "in the power of material historical analysis and a focus on the relationship of class and gender" (Weiler, 2003, p. 272). Feminist reproduction theory focuses on how schooling reproduces existing gender inequalities grounded in Marxist ideology of a connection between schooling and the paid labor force. Women's oppression is reproduced in schools and is represented in the paid workforce and domestic work. Social reproduction is defined as "the reproduction of relationships to and control over economic production and work" (p. 273). The concern here is with how schools "work ideologically to prepare girls to accept their role as low paid or unpaid workers in capitalism" (p. 273). Rosemary Deem echoed this by stating,

> . . . it is clear from almost all the chapters that the reproduction in schooling of gender categories, of class, of the sexual division of labor, of the relations of patriarchy, plays a significant part in the maintenance of the subordinate position of women in our society, whether in paid work, public life or the family. (1980, p.11)

In their research on authority patterns and staffing, Kelly and Nihlen (1982) found a decline of women in higher paying and higher status jobs from the 1950s through the 1970s. Kelly and Nihlen describe girls' display of resistance by enrolling in higher education, although primarily in community colleges. Women construct their identities "through different definitions of what it means to be a woman from their families, their peers, the school, the media, . . . and that this involves both contradictions and conflict" (Weiler, 2003, p. 279). Anyon (1983) argued that women employ a "simultaneous process of accommodation and resistance" (Cited in Weiler, 2003, p. 289). The line is not always clear whether "exaggerated feminine behavior or acquiescence to school authority can be viewed as accommodation or resistance" (p. 289). Cloward and Piven (1979) suggested that "the failure of girls and women to participate in public antisocial groups and activities is the result of a certain psychological tendency to turn opposition and anger inward in private, self-destructive activities" (Cited in Weiler, 2003, p. 290). Women gain power by utilizing different roles. To excel in higher educational leadership, women must negotiate the interplay of power between leaders, peers, and subordinates, perhaps employing different types of accommodation and resistance.

Although the critical perspective is a common way of viewing feminism, poststructural theory adds depth to the nature of construction of gender identity. Poststructuralism suggest that within organizations, systems of speech, symbols and practices divide and "provide a cultural curriculum that disciplines participants to the meaning of institutional categories" (Davidson, 1994, p. 336). Davidson asserts that "meanings are enforced in the context of relationships as individuals, and in the attempt to make sense of each other, attempt to force others into patterns of normative behavior" (p. 336). Julia Kristeva, a French psychoanalyst philosopher, described these generations of feminism in light of poststructuralism.

## KRISTEVA'S POSTSTRUCTURAL VIEW OF FEMINISM

Julia Kristeva was the only woman philosopher in the 1960's and 1970's to usher in poststructuralism alongside Foucault and Derrida. Poststructuralism looks at systems diachronically through process and time using history, process, change, and events, and Kristeva's writings focused on issues of gender and postmodernism. Kristeva's writings were overshadowed by the works of Jacques Derrida, who created a way to "deconstruct" language, but Kristeva's unique contribution was to "dynamize" the structure by considering "the speaking subject and its unconscious experience on the one hand and, on the other, the pressures of other social structures" (McAfee, 2004, p. 7).

Kristeva focused on subjectivity where the subject is shaped by all kinds of phenomena: their culture, relationships, language, history, and contexts. Subjects are not aware of these phenomena and this dimension is unconscious (McAfee, 2004). McAfee stated that "instead of seeing language as a tool used by selves, those who use the term 'subjectivity' understand that language helps produce subjects" (p. 2). Kristeva believed that linguistically the signifying process has two modes: the semiotic and the symbolic. The semiotic is the extra-verbal way in which bodily energy, including the subject's drives, is reflected through language. Although much of the non-verbal communication of body position, gestures, and visceral energy that is associated with movement was not available via recorded tape in this research (Behar-Horenstein & Sigel, 1999), the semiotic in language is emotive and makes itself felt. The transcribed data is a representation of the symbolic which is the sign system complete with grammar and syntax; however, the semiotic can be discharged into the symbolic and thus the dichotomies are intertwined (McAfee, 2004). Scientists attempt to communicate through symbolic language with as little ambiguity as possible while artists use expressions that exemplify the semiotic (McAfee, 2004). The semiotic and symbolic in combination produces types of discourse and cultural practices.

In *Women's Time,* Kristeva describes three generations of European feminism. By generations, Kristeva means "less a chronology than a signifying space, a mental space that is at once corporeal and desirous" (1995, p. 222). The first space is located prior to 1968, where women sought all the rights and privileges that men had. Women deserved equal rights because they were "just like" men; there were no important differences between genders. These feminists' goal was to "inhabit the time of linear history, where women's accomplishments could be inserted in the linear timeline of human history" (McAfee, 2004, p. 93). Women's time in the household was not linear but cyclical—cleaning, sleeping, and birthing, where nothing new is created, just recreated. Kristeva's women's time is a reflection of Martin's reproductive processes.

In 1980, Kristeva stated that women's protest must be more than for the equality of rights, but must consist "in demanding that attention be paid to the subjective, particularly that an individual represents in the social order, of course, but also and above all in relation to what essentially differentiates that individual which is the individual's sexual difference" (Guberman, 1996, p. 116). What distinguishes women from men is not just biological, but it is also the social and symbolic orders that create the dimensions of a larger system. Kristeva suggests that "women's demands cannot be met by identifying with the system or by asking the system to identify with them" (McAfee, 2004, p. 96).

After 1968, feminists looked to clarify the differences between men and women in respect to power, language, and meaning (Kristeva, 1995). While the first generation diminished difference, the second generation began to emphasize revaluing all that is feminine. This included a rejection of male linear timeline and a return to cyclical time and an embrace of motherhood but with continued demands for equality; "instead of seeking to be producers in a linear history, they have sought ways to revalue the lives of women as upholders of the species" (McAfee, 2005, p. 98). The danger of the second generation's revolt lies in the fact that sometimes, "by fighting against evil, we reproduce it, this time at the core of the social bond - the bond between men and women" (Kristeva, 1995, p. 214). Creating a counterculture leads to a kind of reverse sexism that erases women's individuality.

With a rejection of the essentialist first and second waves of feminism, came the embrace of poststructural theory throughout the 1980's and 1990's. This essentialist construction of feminine subjectivity "gave way to one celebrating identity politics based on kaleidoscopic difference and diversity, hybridity and multiplicity" (Luke, 2001, p. 11). The intention of the third generation is to "combine the sexual with the symbolic in order to discover first the specificity of the feminine and then the specificity of each woman" (Kristeva, 1995, p. 210). This generation gives balance to the reproductive and productive desires of women where they can reconcile the need to have children and a career. Women can be "both reproducers of the species and producers of culture" (McAfee, 2004, p. 100). In the first two generations, the choice always seemed to be the self-abnegating activity of motherhood versus the self-affirming activity of culture. Now:

> If maternity is to be guilt-free, this journey needs to be undertaken without masochism and without annihilating one's affective, intellectual, and professional personality, either. In this way, maternity becomes a true creative act, something that we have not yet been able to imagine. (Kristeva, 1995, p.220)

The goal is to internalize the rivalries of the difference thus celebrating the individualism of each person's identity that "patches together a diversity of ethnic, regional, sexual, professional, and political identifications" (McAfee, 2004, p. 102). This practice is consistent with the poststructural focus of Kristeva on diversity of identification and the relativity of our symbolic and biologic selves. In conclusion, the third generation is less about gaining rights and more about gains for all humans. This rejection of metanarratives and universalisms coincides with the cultural changes evident in globalization (Luke, 2001). Instead of "patriarchy" being the culprit for oppression of women, the responsibility lies equally on all human beings who are both "equally guilty- and equally capable of bringing about a new ethical vision" (McAfee, 2004, p. 102). Gender difference becomes not "masochistic or constraining, but, rather, productive and freeing for women and their sexuality" (McAfee, 2004, p. 103). Rather than focusing on the hierarchies of male versus female, the goal is to recognize our internal rivalries and sweep off our side of the street first.

Kristeva's important works included a book about political philosopher Hannah Arendt, who analyzed the life of Jewess Rahel Varnhagen. Rahel (1771-1833) was a product of Jewish social affluence, benefiting from the philo-Semitism of Fredric II of Prussia and later facing the hostility of the nobility class. The new regime of 1810, which professed Enlightenment ideals of equality, also rekindled latent anti-Semitism. Rahel was passionate about literature and philosophy and maintained one of the most fascinating romantic salons, frequented by such famous people as Prince Louis-Ferdinand of Russia, the Humbolt brothers, and even Goethe. Kristeva's book, *Hannah Arendt*, attempted to show aspects of "the manner in which assimilation to the intellectual and social life of the environment works out concretely in the history of an individual's life, thus shaping a personal destiny" (Kristeva, 2001, p. 53). Arendt interpreted Rahel's fate as a view of a "failed assimilation" (p. 53). This failure was from the perspective of being Jewish in a cultural era of Catholicism and Enlightenment universalism. Arendt suggested that Rahel's struggle against the fact of being born Jewish became a struggle against herself, and that Rahel's illusion is her belief that her guests "authenticate her even though in truth they are utterly indifferent to her" (p. 57). Rahel eventually changed to a German name and was baptized; however, all her social actions failed to integrate her into the German nation, and panicked by her lack of assimilation Rahel asked, "Can one get entirely away from what one truly is?" (Weissberg, 1997, p. 243)

This psychosocial depiction demonstrates the impact when people deviate outside the cultural norm. Women in leadership positions assimilate into a masculine world. An example of the effects of assimilation is revealed by professional women who suffer from internal conflict regarding family obligations. Women decide whether to prioritize career over other pursuits such as motherhood and caring for their family, choices that do not traditionally impact men. Kristieva's contribution to feminism and on the effect of a contradictory discourse on women's identities is important to the context of this study.

## SUMMARY

Research has traditionally been conducted primarily by men, and the "results to some extent bear the imprint of certain male-tinted assumptions, priorities, foci and even scientific ideas and methodologies" (Alvesson & Skoldberg, 2001, p. 212). The dominating rules of science are part of patriarchal domination, and a feminist standpoint of research is legitimated by "women's concrete experiences of discrimination and repression" (Alvesson & Skoldberg, p. 230). "Feminism as a Western social movement has had a profound influence on the daily lives of women and men by challenging patriarchy at every turn" (St. Pierre & Pillow, 2000, pg. 2). Discrimination and patriarchy influence the environment that women leaders negotiate through forms of resistance and accommodation. However, women of the third generation seek to balance the dichotomy between their reproductive and productive desires.

# Chapter Three

# Philosophy of Practice

## EPISTEMOLOGY AND THEORETICAL FRAMEWORK

The previous chapter provided an overview of feminism and its historical foundations which has formed systems of power and knowledge in educational institutions. The ambiguous nature of feminist poststructuralism requires a review of the theoretical foundations and methods which form the basis of this research. Poststructuralism adopts difference, heterogeneity, fragmentation, shifting identities of subjects and the absence of certainty; there is a lack of decidability of interpretation (Schwandt, 2001). This theoretical perspective embraces abstract methodologies such as rhizoanalysis and deconstruction as research strategies. Although poststructuralism lacks the definitiveness of modernist approaches, the methodology and methods using this perspective can be grounded theoretically.

Epistemology (how we know what we know) is the theory of knowledge that is embedded in the theoretical perspective and in the methodology (Crotty, 1998). Modernism has great faith in the ability to discover absolute forms of knowledge, while postmodern approaches refuse all essentialist orientations of modernist thought. The quest for certainty, characteristic of an objectivist epistemology, has been thought to be a futile and dysfunctional search. A subjectivist epistemology versus objectivism commits to "ambiguity, relativity, fragmentation, particularity, and discontinuity. . . . one is the antithesis of the other" (Crotty, 1998, p.185). Hargreaves suggests that using subjectivism involves "denying the existence of foundational knowledge on the grounds that no knowable social reality exists beyond the signs of language, image, and discourse" (1994, p. 39). Language forges the immersion of discourse. A poststructuralist approach characterizes differences found in signs of language, image and discourse.

26

Post-structuralism emerged out of an intellectual movement that was dissatisfied with the confines of structuralism, a movement based on Saussurean linguistics, and is linked to the work of the French writers, Foucault, Lyotard, Derrida, and Kristeva (Craib, 1992; Grogan, 2003; Sarup, 1988). Post-structualists believe that, "language, meaning, social institutions and the self are destabilized" (Palmer, 1998, p. 145). Discourse is the vehicle that guides this process. The prevalent patriarchal discourse is characterized by individualism, hierarchy, impersonality, and competition (Alvesson & Skoldberg, 2001). Discourse is described as an intersubjective phenomenon that "is not a direct product of subjectivity and has a constituent role in the production of the symbolic systems that govern human existence" (Macey, 2000, p.100). This definition of discourse was based on Foucault's discursive formation, which he described as "homogeneous fields of enunciative regularities" (Foucault, 1972/2002, p. 117). For Foucault, "relations of force and power are involved at every level of a discursive formation; . . . knowledge is always a form of power" (Macey, 2000, p. 101). Discursive practices are a:

Body of anonymous, historical rules, always determined in the time and space that have defined a given period, and for a given social, economic, geographical, or linguistic area, the conditions of operation of the enunciative function. (Foucault, 1972/2002, p. 117)

Deconstructionism is "a poststructural strategy for reading texts that unmasks the supposed 'truth' or meaning of text by undoing, reversing, and displacing taken-for-granted binary oppositions that structure texts (e.g., right over wrong, subject over object, reason over nature, men over women, speech over writing, and reality over appearance)" Schwandt, 2001, p. 203-4). While there are inherent dualisms in the text, deconstruction destabilizes the binaries. Instead of a hierarchical pyramid where the top tier oppresses the others, the focus is the contextual interaction between individuals and institutions.

## RHIZOME

This study deconstructed the concept of women's leadership using rhizo-analysis to unfold the connections between the binaries. The rhizome "has no beginning or end; it is always in the middle, between things, intervening, intermezzo" (Deleuze & Guattari, 1980/1987, p. 25). A rhizome is an underground tuber that diverges into new places.

A rhizome ceaselessly establishes connections between semiotic chains, organizations of power, and circumstances relative to the arts, sciences, and social struggles. A semiotic chain is like a tuber agglomerating very diverse acts, no only linguistic, but also perceptive, mimetic, gestural, and cognitive. (Deleuze & Guattari, 1980/1987, p. 7)

Rhizoanalyisis emphasizes on how texts function outside of themselves as they connect with other contexts, beliefs, and readers. The image is of the nomad deterritorializing consciously structured striated space. Deleuze and Guattari use these spaces together; "smooth space is constantly being translated, transversed into a striated space; striated space is constantly being reversed, returned into a smooth space" (1980/1987, p. 474). Nomadic researchers travel to smooth spaces as they always possess a "greater power of deterritorialization than the striated" (p. 480). As a researcher, my personal experiences and readings connected the findings into new areas of thought. St. Pierre explained that, "a nomadic ethnographer speeding within connections and conduits and multiplicities might gnaw a smooth space to extend her territory" (St. Pierre & Pillow, 2000, p. 264).

The image of the fold helps the researcher think differently (St. Pierre, 1997). The fold disrupts the notion of interiority, since it defines "the inside as the operation of the outside" (Deleuze, 1986/1988, p. 97). The folds function is to avoid the simplistic reversal of binaries, and its function is to "avoid distinction, opposition, fatal binarity" (Badiou, 1994, p. 61). The fold seeks the middle and avoids extremes and opposites. Although the language of the participants unfolded a binary discourse, my task was to search for contradictions in the text as discrepancies collapsed on each other. "What matters is folding, unfolding, refolding" (Deleuze, 1988/1993, p. 137). In this context, this study looked for how the identities of the participants unfolded within the hierarchical binaries of the social strata.

Derrida expanded these post-structural concepts with deconstruction. "The very meaning and mission of deconstruction is to show that things-texts, institutions, traditions, societies, beliefs, and practices of whatever size and sort you need-do not have definable meanings and determinable missions, that they are always more than any mission would impose, that they exceed the boundaries they currently occupy" (Caputo, 1997, p. 31). Derrida believed that logocentric reasoning privileges one of two sides of binary opposites, and that, "the prioritizing of one pole over the other displays mere cultural manipulations of power, and to show that, under deconstructive scrutiny, these oppositions break down and collapse into each other" (Palmer, 1998, p. 134). For example, democracies are constantly evolving and may represent the best form of government, but they are corrupted by money, politicians, and the media, often undermining the poor and defenseless via the hypocrisy under the guise of reform (Caputo, 1997). Deconstruction seeks to question those revered things by exposing the most venerable to attack. Deconstruction is "nourished by a dream of the invention of the other, of something to come, something absolutely unique and idiomatic, the invention, the in-coming, of an absolute surprise" (Caputo, 1997, p. 70).

Such blurring of context is deconstruction's mission. Deconstruction desires "straight" men to get in touch with their feminine side, and "straight" women get in touch with their masculine side (Caputo, 1997, p. 104). In Derrida's view, "male" and "female" are fixed containers that close off the possibility of "innumerable" genders, not just two" (Caputo, 1997, p. 104-5). While feminism provides a "necessary moment of "reversal," a salutary overturning that purges the system of its present masculinist hegemony, it must give way to "displacement," and "gender bending" in which the whole "masculine/feminine schema is skewed" (Caputo, 1997, p. 105). So Derrida's term *différance*, is the interplay of difference where as researchers "search for meaning, therefore, we are sent to difference, and meaning is deferred" (Crotty, 1998, p. 207). *Différance* captures the twin significance of difference and deferral. Every element of discourse is bears "the trace within it of other elements in the chain, so that everywhere there are differences of differences and traces of traces" (Derrida, 1981, p. 26).


## POSTSTRUCTURAL INTERVIEWING

Interviewing was used to gain understanding of participants' identity construction. We are in an "interview society" (Silverman, 1998, p. 126), where mass media, researchers, and service providers generate endless information through interviewing. Historically, individuality did not exist in a recognizable social form (Gubrium & Holstein, 2003). After WWII, the interview changed with the emergence of the standardized survey where individuals became accustomed to offering information to strangers. It was recognized that each person had a voice, thus there was a "democratization of opinion" (Gubrium & Holstein, 2003, p. 22). This view stemmed from William James, who in 1892, noted that every individual has a sense of self that is owned and controlled by him, even if the self is socially formulated and interpersonally responsive (Holstein & Gubrium, 2003). All interviews are interactional conversations that vary from highly structured survey interviews to free-flowing exchanges (Silverman, 1998).

The outcome to research on the democratization of opinion through the survey was part of a trend of "increased surveillance in every day life" (Gubrium & Holstein, 2003, p. 24). Foucault's studies on the changed the concept of individuality. The institutional contexts ranging from the medical clinic to the prison showed us how the "technologies of the self" transformed the view of subjectivity (Foucault, 1988). Foucault's "technologies of the self" are the concrete, socially and historically located institutional practices which constructs our individuality (Foucault, 1988). Subjectivity suggests a morally responsible agent behind the participant's words and actions, such as the family, tribe, community or institution (Gubrium & Holstein, 2003). Postmodernists treat interviewing as a place in which knowledge is constructed, and suggest that the interview is not a neutral "conduit," but a "place of producing reportable knowledge itself" (Silverman, 1998, p.114).

The post-modern perspective suggests that the researcher and participants have multiple intentions and desires, some of which are conscious and some of which are not. The poststructural perspective sees language as slippery and ambiguous; sign and signification are only loosely linked (Saussure, 1949/1983). What a question or answer means to the interviewee may change, and what occurs in a specific interview is contingent on the specifics of individuals, place, and time (Mishler, 1986). Changing the interviewer changes the results, even if the new interviewer asks the same questions.

Scheurich (1995) agrees that interviewing is characterized by asymmetries of power, but suggests an alternative view. With the power inequities, there is resistance as described by critical theorists such as Apple, Giroux, Weiler, and Freire. However, the less powerful "find innumerable, creative, even powerful ways to resist inequity" (Weiler, 1988, p. 21). Weiler suggests that "individuals are not simply acted upon by abstract 'structures' but negotiate, struggle, and create meaning of their own" (p. 21). Interviewees control part of the interview and "use the interviewer as much as the interviewer uses the interviewees" (Scheurich, 1995, p. 247). Scheurich replaces the critical binary with an open-ended third space he calls "chaos." Resistance persists as long as dominance persists, therefore "in the interview the aims of the researcher may not be met by the participants" (Scheurich, 1995, p. 248).

The interview interaction is a complex play of conscious and unconscious thoughts, feelings, fears, and needs on the part of both the interviewer and interviewee that cannot be categorized—no stable "reality" can be represented (p. 249). This interpretive moment occurs throughout the research process as "a plethora of baggage" (p. 249). During the interview with women administrators, there were allowances for the "uncontrollable play of power within the interaction," (p. 250) and the juxtaposition of power that occurred. Although they have power as given by their positions, the power interchange was equalized by the presence of my tape recorder and their "knowing" that my analysis might be different than their own perspective of themselves.

## PARTICIPANTS AND SETTING

Ten women administrators were interviewed in their offices on campus at a research one university in the Southeastern United States. Interviewees were selected using the criterion sampling method on the basis of their length of service as administrators and willingness to participate. Interviewees all had been in a supervisory position in higher education for at least three years. Five interviewees were full deans and five were associate deans. Five women were from historically male-dominated fields and the five others from female-dominated fields and/or colleges. A male-dominated (MD) versus female-dominated (FD) field is defined as a college within the university system with greater than 50% male or female faculty respectively. The following table depicts the participants' pseudonyms and general attributes.

| Pseudonyms | College | Dean or Associate |
|---|---|---|
| Abe | MD | Associate |
| Bennett | FD | Associate |
| Dare | MD | Dean |
| Dunlap | FD | Associate |
| Emmett | FD | Dean |
| Highe | MD | Dean |
| Langer | FD | Dean |
| Sasser | MD | Associate |
| Vitalia | MD | Dean |
| Wilson | FD | Associate |

Confidentiality was adhered to according to the University of Florida's IRB guidelines and policies. Participants' privacy and anonymity was respected and protected by the researcher by using pseudonyms in all writings. Correspondence was limited to direct contact with participants via mail, telephone or e-mail. These procedures reflect the researcher's sensitivity toward interviewees and prevented any harm from their participation in this study. I had no previous contact with the interviewees to avert prejudgment and to create an unbiased presence during the interviews.

## DATA COLLECTION METHODS

Using a semi-structured interview approach, campus-based interviews ranged from 45-100 minutes in duration. Written consent was obtained. All tapes were transcribed by professional transcribers, and then reviewed and corrected by the researcher. The transcriptions were member checked by the participants for validation purposes. Interview questions included:

1. Can you give me some background information?
2. What made you a leader?

3. What is leadership?
4. How has your self been changed as a result of your leadership?
5. What differences does being a woman make in your leadership?
6. Describe the influences of power on your leadership?
7. How do you use and produce power?
8. How has your leadership changed?
9. Describe a situation that best illustrates your leadership.
10. Is there anything that you would like to add?


## VALIDITY AND TRUSTWORTHINESS

Validity has also been referred to as "trustworthiness" (Denzin & Lincoln, 2000, p. 230). Means of assessing trustworthiness or research validity continues throughout the research design as well as in the midst of data collection. Some conventional tools used to enhance the validity in this study included triangulation, peer review and debriefing, negative case analysis, clarification of researcher bias, member checking, search for negative cases, rich, thick description, and external audit (Creswell, 1998). However, a feminist post-structural perspective requires unique considerations. Richardson proposed a transgressive form of validity by examining the properties of a crystal in a metaphoric sense:

> I propose that the central imaginary for "validity" for postmodernist texts is not the triangle--a rigid, fixed, two-dimensional object. Rather the central imaginary is the crystal, which combines symmetry and substance with an infinite variety of shapes, substances, transmutations, multidimensionalities, and angles of approach. Crystals grow, change, alter, but are not amorphous. Crystals are prisms that reflect externalities and refract within themselves, creating different colors, patterns, arrays, casting off in different directions. . . . Crystallization, without losing structure, deconstructs the traditional idea of "validity" (we feel how there is no single truth, we see how texts validate themselves); and crystallization provides us with a deepened, complex, thoroughly partial understanding of the topic. Paradoxically, we know more and doubt what we know. (1997, p. 92)

Lather also seeks a "transgressive" validity that is disruptive for the status quo which purposes to "rupture validity as a regime of truth, to displace its historical inscription . . . via a catalytic validity or a proliferation of counter-practices of authority that take the crisis of representation into account" (1993, p. 674). Lather also described validty in a Derridean rigor/rhizomatic context, "via relay, multiple openings; networks, and complexities of problematics;" and a voluptuous/situated validity which "embodies a situated, partial tentativeness," "constructs authority via practices of engagement and self-reflexivity," and "brings ethics and epistemology together" (1993, p. 686).

The crisis of representation conceives that no interpretive account can capture lived experience which, combined with the crisis of legitimation, challenges the authority of the interpretive text, and creates a crisis of praxis-conclusion (Denzin & Lincoln, 2000). The definition of this last crisis is that if society is only and always a text, no definitive conclusions can be made to create social and political reform. This triple crisis occurred in the 1980's where conventional validity verification procedures were re-theorized to include those of Richardson and Lather. These ideas challenge beliefs in each social science discipline about the frameworks that guide empirical research.

My subjective reflexivity influenced this study by my own experience as a reorganized manager in the for-profit healthcare sector and by the 2003 suicide of my sister, a clinical neurologist, who failed to gain tenure in a top-tier medical school. These experiences disrupted my previous views of the leadership "regime of truth" and provided impetus for this study (Foucault, 1984, p. 74). My interpretations of the data were transformed by my bereavement, but my own management experiences also unfolded the complexities of leadership. As the fold seeks the middle and avoids extremes and opposites, my task was to search for contradictions and discrepancies in the text as they collapsed on each other. However, my purpose was clear; I was driven to comprehend the dynamics of women leaders in large hierarchical institutions.

## SUMMARY

Finding the patterns of discourse, subjectivity, resistance, power and knowledge was the purpose for this feminist poststructural study. There has been little written about women administrators in higher education using this theoretical framework. Poststructuralism lends a perspective of questioning, emphasizes the need for the understanding between power and knowledge, and focuses on the microhistories of individual lives. As the binaries unfolded within the text, the contradictions were deconstructed in search of the middle; thus expanding the understanding of leadership to include different dimensionalities and counter-practices of authority.

# Chapter Four

# Results

## IDENTITIES BECOMING

Binary oppositions (men/women, best/worst) are common in modern society. Deleuze and Guattari (1987) see humans as assigned to different strata in play, work, social structure, and household tasks. Organizations compartmentalize themselves into an entire bureaucracy that is rigidly segmented and centralized and resembles an arborescent hierarchical system which disciplines and controls the appendages (or divisions) attached to it. These appendages represent personnel with a multiplicity of departmental duties that interconnect together as a rhizome. St. Pierre stated that, "it is the outside that folds us into identity, and we can never control the forces of the outside" (2000, p. 260). My interest focused on how these women leaders constructed, "their subjectivitities within the limits and possibilities of the discourses and cultural practices that are available to them" (p. 258).

In research, the question commonly raised is, "What did you find?" The researcher is then compelled to discuss his or her research in search of oppositions in a pyramidal structure of results. I struggled for months to avoid these structured striated spaces that pervade the dominant positivistic realm of scientific inquiry. However, I repeatedly returned to sedentary, striated spaces which are coded, bounded, and limited (St. Pierre, 2000), allured by the participants' language such as "define," "most," and "typical" to produce categories. As a former administrator, I identified with the language of the participants, and so when analyzing the interviews I was drawn to categorize participants' distinguishing characteristics. The typical interviewee was Caucasian, had children, was divorced and remarried in a stable relationship. Several had married young and then as their education advanced had divorced, and now had a very supportive spouse.

34

The text illustrated that the identities of these women as "leaders" were embedded in the masculine discursive voice. However, this type of analysis of these inside/outside binaries led to failure when attempting to find the deconstructive "middle." This "practice of failure" transformed, my "impossibility into possibility where a failed account occasions new kinds of positioning" (Lather, 1996, p. 3). Over the course of several months, I slowly decoded the striated spaces and realized "smooth space and striated space do not exist in opposition but in mixture" (St. Pierre, 2000, p. 264). Deleuze and Guattari use these spaces together; "smooth space is constantly being translated, transversed into a striated space; striated space is constantly being reversed, returned into a smooth space" (1980/1987, p. 474). "Identities becoming" describe how the participants' identities comply, deviate, and shift in their social realms as leaders in their organizations.

Using the rhizome to analyze the meaning of the textual language extends the boundaries of what is considered knowledge. Julia Kristeva's writings considered the speaking subject and their unconscious experience and compared that to the pressures of other social structures (McAfee, 2004). Kristeva believed that linguistically the signifying process included the semiotic, which is the extra-verbal way in which bodily energy, including the subject's drives, is reflected through language. These women deans are shaped by their subjectivities which include their culture, relationships, language, history, and contexts. Because of my interest in poststructural theories, I used the texts of these deans to explore these "women's arts of existence, or practices of the self, the things they do every day that make them who they are" (St. Pierre, 2005, p. 1). The textual focus was to consider the speaking subjects and determine their unconscious experiences in the social structure of educational leadership.

Deterritorialized identities, becoming masculine, becoming feminine, becoming powerful, becoming powerless, becoming stereotypes, and becoming difference: "that is what multiplicity is" (Deleuze & Guattari, 1987, p. 32). The "becoming" multiplicities are real "even if that something other it becomes is not" (p. 32). For clarification, a becoming lacks a subject distinct from itself. Deleuze and Guattari compare it to the rhizome in this way:

> Becoming is a rhizome, not a classificatory or genealogical tree. Becoming is certainly not imitating, or identifying with something: neither is it regressing-progressing; neither is it corresponding, establishing corresponding relations; neither is it producing, producing a filiation or producing through filiation. Becoming is a verb with a consistency all its own; it does not reduce to, lead back to, "appearing," "being," "equaling," or "producing." (Deleuze & Guattari, 1987, p. 239)

This excerpt demonstrates that it is easier to understand what "becoming" is not, rather than what it is. A line of becoming "is not defined by points that it connects, or by points that compose it; . . . it passes *between* points, it comes up through the middle. . . . (and) has only a middle" (Deleuze and Guattari, 1987, p. 293). The lines of becoming (see Appendix A) are the shades of gray between black and white- not either/or, but the "middle" of any extreme. The "middle" is a part of each which unfolds to the next "middle." Because of my subjectivity related to the term "leadership," the image of the fold helped me view the leadership binaries differently. The fold disrupts the notion of interiority, since it defines "the inside as the operation of the outside" (Deleuze, 1986/1988, p. 97). The fold's function is to avoid the simplistic reversal of binaries. "What matters is folding, unfolding, refolding" (Deleuze, 1988/1993, p. 137). The "identity" sections examine how the identities of the participants unfolded between the hierarchical binaries of the social strata.

## IDENTITY OF THE MASCULINE

In a social strata of the masculine binary, Porter (1989) viewed leaders as people who created followers' roles, rewarded proficiency, negotiated obstacles, promoted interaction, and created coalitions for institutional problem solving. The deans used these characteristics to describe themselves even at a young age. As children these women organized their friends to do all kinds of activities. Most were outgoing, but even if they were shy individuals, they had an incessant need to coordinate tasks to achieve some goal -- and they loved doing it.

One dean in a male-dominated college described this trait this way:

> *Given a set of circumstances, I can organize people, I can get us to do things as a team, that's what I like to do, and in the hopes of achieving something and I think that °piece is always important.° You know I wasn't going to be a baton twirler if we couldn't be state champions. . . . At the same (time) . . . if you don't want to practice, then you're not going to be on my team because you're not going to share that dream of being a state champion.*

The language of the text was filled with achievement and hierarchy—of rising higher than others. Even in a traditional female-dominated activity of baton twirling, this participant desired her teammates to join in her dream of being state champions or face exclusion. Years later, she became a dean of a male-dominated college and continued that precedent. Another dean illustrated this need for achievement as, "looking to go up" in regards to her career. Associate Dean Abe described her rise into leadership as "sometimes you have to just pick up the ball and run yourself." This text resembles the game metaphors that Joseph Crowley (1994), in a historical study on college presidents, associated with leadership including words such as titan, hero, gladiator, and quarterback. The deans organized others toward a goal to be the best in whatever they were doing. If others did not have the same goal, they needed to go elsewhere.

## IDENTITY OF THE FEMININE

These women rose to the top of their professional organizations early in their careers and honed their leadership skills. Dean Highe spoke of being on, "campus wide committees on budget and personnel and planning . . . you know, I loved it." This "love" of organization and planning was a common descriptor used by the deans. These feminine expressions portrayed their enthusiasm for their roles and were interspersed within the predominant masculine discourse. Another dean described her interactions with people as searching the "environment of what's the sort of emotional content, what's resonating against" the situation. Her scrutiny of the emotional aspects of situations, and then the use of the language of "resonate" represents an application of feminine language into the text. Another dean perceived her position as a "service" job where she was promoted because of her drive toward the "greater good." Feminine descriptors like "service" and "greater good" were interposed within the masculine leadership discourse of these deans.

Subjectivity stems from the concept that discourses systematically "form the objects of which they speak" (Sarup, 1988, p. 70). Therefore, a man or woman who becomes an administrator is shaped or subjectified by that discourse. These women used predominately masculine language with some inclusion of feminine language. Even the deans in women-dominated colleges were surrounded by male-mentors who directed them. Although these women grew up during the time of the second wave of the women's movement, their primary mentors and predecessors were male. These women's language reflected the discourse of their environment as the outside folded them into their identities. These women constructed "their subjectivitities within the limits and possibilities of the discourses and cultural practices that are available to them" (St. Pierre, 2000, p. 258).

## IDENTITY OF THE FATHER

These women identified their families as an important part of their cultural practices. Dean Langer talked about how fortunate she was because her family "celebrates" her successes by putting her press releases on their refrigerators.

This kind of encouragement from their families sustained the deans' enthusiasm about their work. Although these women spoke of children, husbands, and other relatives, most gave an account about their parents. Regarding this Dean Langer stated,

> . . . ° it maybe has gotten me into trouble sometimes. I'm a bit too outspoken.°
> (. . .) I actually think it came from a combination of my mother and my father.
> Because I can see parts of their personalities that I got and I'm not sort of a clone
> of either one of them, but I got some, (. . .) remarkably positive characteristics
> from each of them and I was lucky in that regard.

This dean believed that her strength comes from positive characteristics from both her parents. Her identity is not cloned, but is a mixture of theirs. Although she apologized initially for her boldness, she then described this attribute as "remarkably positive" even as her husband recoiled. Her identity was not entirely shaped by her immediate environment, but evolved from her parents.

Of their parents, these women spoke at length about their fathers as their first mentors who, "believed that education was the ticket to a better life." These women understood how fortunate they were to have fathers who believed in education equally for their daughters as well as for their sons. Dean Vitalia described her father in this way.

> *My father was my first mentor. (. . .) He did treat my sister and I different than*
> *he treated our brother. (Laughter) It's just he couldn't help it. You know? (. . .)*
> *But, Daddy was very, always very, very encouraging and supportive and (. . .)*
> *whatever you put your mind to, you can do.*

Dean Vitalia attributed her success to her father, but recognized that her father treated her brother differently. When she decided to go into education, he remarked that it was a "good" profession for women. Her father encouraged her to develop her career and become well-educated; however, he still tied gender roles to careers. Historically, women deans at the turn of the twentieth century had strong relationships with their fathers and other male relatives who were willing educate their daughters during a time when college attendance was not commonplace for women; these relationships gave these early pioneers alliances for their leadership positions (Brown, 2001). The importance of fathers was evident in this associate dean's story.

> *And I adored my father. My father was wonderful as far as encouraging me. He,*
> *he was the one who really supported women. (. . .) He'd become an officer in*
> *the Navy but he'd never graduated from high school. And so recognized, he had*
> *always felt inferior, being in the position and not having the educational back-*

*ground. That's why education was so important to him and why he was willing*
*to pay for me to go to (professional) school (. . . .)*

This dean wore her father's ring during the interview, and reported that the
"foundation" for her life was her father. In her early adult years during the feminist seventies, her mother's role as a homemaker annoyed her. Later, she realized
that her mother's job was to care for her father, which transformed her annoyance
into acceptance of her mother's familial role. This was one of the rare moments
that a mother was mentioned in the text. The support of their fathers and the
women's movement gave these deans other choices, but their lives were incongruent with those of their mothers and a source of conflict. These deans lacked
women role models at all levels as they ascended into their careers and their early
identities were imprinted by their fathers. Therefore, their interactions within the
masculine discourse were influenced by their male relationships.

On the other hand, not all the participants had a supportive family. Sometimes their negative experiences in the family gave them leadership abilities.
One dean reported that she learned responsibility early in her life because of
caring for her infirm mother that compelled her to "take charge of the household." This duty was forced on her because of being the first-born child. Only
one dean expressed extreme dislike for her father, and this disdain influenced
her leadership. Associate Dean Bennett's father was controlling, and in reaction she was determined never to be like him.

> Well, you know, I still bristle at that word power. (. . .) I don't think I've ever had
> anyone be dictatorial so I'm trying to think where it comes from and it probably
> comes from the family. My father was a career military. We had to say, yes, sir,
> no, sir, without question. If we didn't we were slapped, physically. // And so, as
> soon as I was 18 I left home. I wasn't gonna be told what to do nor was I gonna
> fit into a box that my father thought I should fit into.

Her reaction to her father had a big impact on her leadership and her perceptions of power. Dean Bennett associated the term "power" with "bristle" in
very strong language that signified her dictatorial father. She stated that her
style of leadership evolved in opposition to what her father represented to
her. In another text, Dean Bennett was drawn to administration because of
the "power position" where people "would take my call because they knew
who I was," and which she called "fun." She liked being able to select faculty and the power that comes with that authority. Surprisingly, Dean Bennett
later referred to herself as a "control freak," a term that is reminiscent of her
father's control of her. Perhaps unknowingly, she created in herself what she
disdained. The striated space of the importance of her father was reversed to
a smooth space but then unconsciously returned.

## IDENTITY OF THE QUINTESSENCE

The American Heritage Dictionary defines "quintessence" as the "purest, most essential element of a thing" (1994, p. 677). Although these women were influenced by their environment, their journeys into leadership were unfolding extensions of themselves. Only one participant told her dean that, "someday, I would like to be dean," as she was "looking to go up." This sole participant knew she desired the deanship early in her career. Although these women in this study were ambitious, most did not set out to become deans or even leaders. One interviewee stated, "I didn't come into leadership by design . . . and sometimes people with voices of change move into leadership positions because that's where you can probably have the biggest impact." The segmented "leadership" discourse is clear in the text and being an "agent of change" thrust her into leadership, yet for the most part, these women did not intend to become leaders.

Dean Highe explained her evolution into the deanship. She involved herself in professional organizations outside her academic job and soon realized she belonged in administration.

> *I was a department chair for four years and I knew the day I became, within the first week that I became a department chair I realized I had waited too long to do that job ( . . .) But this job is really fun because it taps into all kinds of creative abilities as well as organizational and administrative abilities because this is the level, at least for me, other people have different levels, for me this has been the level where I really have had a chance to make a difference in ways that you can ultimately see the impact. ( . . .)*

Dean Highe loved the diversity of responsibilities and the creativity it entailed, and was motivated by the opportunity to create an impact. These participants consistently used masculine descriptive language like "impact" and "making a difference" in regards to their motivation to become leaders. This language corresponded to the productive directional desires of these women which have traditionally been the realm of men. However, the deans also reversed the masculine discourse with words such as "love," "creative," and "fun," illustrating a feminine contribution to the discourse. Initially, Dean Highe had never thought about wanting a leadership position, and no one helped her identify her potential early in her career or suggested that she enter administration. This participant was not directly mentored into leadership; however, she did the tasks that she loved doing and that unfolded her role. While these women had male mentors, they were not mentored into the leadership and yet they still became deans in an intensely male-dominated environment. Dean Highe reflected during her interview that she had never thought about being a women dean. Her concern was the job and her college, not the fight to get there.

As with all of the interviewees, Dean Highe's identity as a leader started before she became a leader. Dean Highe, like other deans, did not "set out to become" a leader, and this text implies her attitude regarding what "made her" a leader.

> *Other people putting a label on it. (. . .) I just got an idea in my mind about how I wanted to live my life, what I wanted to do with it, how I wanted to relate to other people in the world and at the end of the day, people, you know, tell me you are a leader, what you do as a leader. (. . .) But it isn't because I set out to become "a leader". I think that's an illusive title in some ways anyway just by every leader I've seen or known is different from every other one // and every week now when I go to a bookstore and there's yet another book on leadership, there's yet another variation on a theme, another definition on how to be a leader, what a leader is, and there are some commonalities I mean that seem to be in the definitions and descriptions of leadership, but it wasn't that I set out to do it.*

These deans did not read leadership books to look for their leadership identities. Dean Highe recognized the illusive nature of the title, and the differing leadership styles of those leaders around her. Her responses were very ambiguous regarding stereotyping leaders into male and female types. This text suggested that she was not trained for leadership but emerged into her own identity. She had a vision of what she wanted to be and became that. For these women, "being" came before "doing;" and leadership is a "label" for what they were already doing. In reflection, these women were people who organized others, they were surrounded by male role models who encouraged education but not ascension into leadership, and the essential elements of their identities unfolded them into leaders. The striated spaces translated into smooth spaces; leadership is multidimensional.

## IDENTITY OF THE THIRD GENERATION

Dean Highe used a very masculine discourse in her responses; however, she also added multiple dimensions and complexities beyond a segmented reality. The third generation of feminism represents balance to the productive and reproductive desires of women. Women can be both "reproducers of the species and producers of culture," both the body and the social (McAfee, 2004, p. 100). In the first two generations, the choice always seemed to be the self-abnegating activity of motherhood versus the self-affirming activity of culture. Kristeva spoke of the three generations of feminism that are more a mindset than a chronological order. Before 1968, the first generation of women wanted equality with men, the second embraced the feminine, and the third focused on the balance between the productive and reproductive desires of women. Dean Highe's language also reflected complexities beyond the masculine with words such as "creative," "love," and introduced ways of creating feminine balance. In a society where the masculine model of leadership permeates every institution, these women invented their own smooth spaces and recreated innovative ways to balance their lives.

These women spoke of the importance of family relationships, and Dean Vitalia presented a different description of success.

> I can give you examples of successful moments. (. . .) I would say that my, the, my greatest accomplishment in life is my children. It's not, it's, because my job and my career is not really who I am. It's something that I do.

In the previous section, it was suggested that these women's leadership identities sprang up from their "being." In this excerpt, Dean Vitalia separates her "doing" job from her "being." This unfolds another dimension of her identity where she balanced her productive and reproductive roles. These women seemed content with their personal lives, and most spoke of being in long-term relationships at this point in their careers. Those women with children spoke proudly of them, no differently than other mothers. Their identities were multi-dimensional and their texts suggested that they were not entirely preoccupied with work.

However, not all women spoke of family relationships, and some were not unhappy about being preoccupied by work. Dean Highe was content without a family because she did not have the "pulls and the responsibilities" outside of work, and yet, she did not feel "overly unbalanced" in her early work-life. The women's enjoyment of work grew out of an extension of their personalities. Both Dean Vitalia and Dean Highe expressed contentment and balance, although for different reasons. The literature often speaks of the difficulties that women might have managing family and careers, or portrays focused career women in a negative light (Marshal & Jones, 1990). For example, Shultz and Easter (1997) reported that women administrators have reported homemaking and child care as social barriers to advancement. However, these deans enjoyed and directed their busy lives. They did not complain about their family roles; their lives were what they wanted and were an extension of who they were as individuals.

At one point, Dean Highe described how she mentally balanced these divisions in her life.

> *I'm content about, the job that I'm at, I'm never content about how well we're doing because once you become content, (. . .) then I think that contentment can*

*lead to a complacency that means you're not really raising the bar for what can*
*be gathered in. But there are two bromides that I say to myself every day, one*
*is nothing's perfect and then to help keep me from going nuts, the other is, no-*
*body can do it all.*

This text represents an interchange of language between a masculine discourse of "raising the bar" versus "contentment" which Dean Highe equated complacency. These women used active verbs in their language such as "accomplish," and "make it happen," and then used language to soften the extremes to keep from "going nuts." The deans lived in an environment of hierarchical vertical thinking, and moderated those extremes by reminding themselves that "nobody can do it all." The language represented a folding and unfolding of the striated binaries to the smooth space of the middle.

Dean Dare's interview was a good example of the folding and unfolding between the productive and reproductive needs of these women. She reflected on the dichotomies that motivated her life.

*Well what drives me . . . I mean I think I'm just kind of a compulsive over-*
*achiever, just . . . you know we all have those personal afflictions, but I think*
*what drives me in terms of being . . . doing this job or any of my administrative*
*service oriented jobs, // I think it's just seeing the // shaping the institution or*
*trying to create a greater good and having the opportunity to do that in a posi-*
*tion that allows me to do that which would not have occurred being in a labora-*
*tory, doing my own research.*

Dean Dare described her compulsiveness for achievement as a "personal affliction;" however, she says that administration is a service-oriented job to create a greater good. This is reminiscent of Kirkpatrick's study (1974) of women in state legislatures, where women searched for solutions to serve the common good. When describing what drives her, she first used the word "being" then "doing;" she does the job, but her "being" was driven by "shaping the institution for the greater good." "Driven" represented her productive desires that seemed to conflict with her reproductive sense of service.

The language is fraught with paradoxes: compulsive, over-achiever, personal afflictions, service-oriented, shaping the institution for the greater good. She splits her language and thus her identity into positive and negative traits. Women's "drive" to excel in the cultural arena conflict with women's reproductive, nurturing values creating negative feelings. Perhaps being driven to create a "greater good" sanctions their ambition, or an attitude of service quiets their productive desires so they can balance the productive and reproductive portions of their lives. Dean Dare's leadership ambition was balanced by her need for practicality, impact and meaning. Her described motivation, like the other participants, was for service and not for domination in the hierarchy.

These women reported that money did not motivate them but described a motivating desire to shape their profession. Dean Dare even reports that "I don't know that anyone would do this job for the amount of money they pay you; you have to be driven by something °more than that°." During the interview, the "°more than that°" was spoken quietly as an afterthought, as if she was not sure what motivated her. Dean Dare later laughed at not being the highest paid in her male-dominated college with a hint of resentment. Signs of her need to achieve were always present, but balanced by her reproductive desires. In another excerpt, Dean Dare spoke of "never in a million years" that she would be a dean, but became one because of her motivation "toward the greater good," and the unfolding journey of "just being prepared . . . being asked to do things." In a male-dominated college, Dean Dare performed tasks that men did not want to do for "the greater good."

Associate Dean Abe from a male-dominated college was promoted because she chaired the curriculum committee because, "I usually didn't volunteer for things, but whenever I was asked to do something, I'd always do it." She had felt that the old curriculum was "a disservice for our students." In the early 20th century, women who did not see the need for suffrage sought the vote to alleviate the social ills of society. Dean Highe echoed this emphasis on service by saying, "our first job is to make sure that this is a really good learning experience for students." The nurturing reproductive desires of women have historically motivated them for action.

Dean Vitalia echoed this sentiment of acting for the "greater good" even when it would be detrimental to her personally.

> *If I see me stepping up to say something as going to possibly be detrimental to me, but helpful for the college, then I would have, then I'd, I'll have to, I'll have to say it, because that's my responsibility is to not be looking out for me, but to be looking out for the good and the needs of the college. . . . I think that we have some people in positions of authority now that maybe a little too concerned about themselves, and so they're not necessarily looking out for the greater good.*

Dean Vitalia distinguishes between leaders and authority by examining their motivation; whether they have concern for themselves or for the "greater good." The deans were acutely aware of those in authority who they considered to be "too concerned" in regards to themselves. Brunner (2005) reported that women superintendents were uncomfortable using power over other people and desired empowerment for the greater good. The motivation of these women reverberated around the reproductive desires of the feminine.

Although these women lived and functioned within striated masculine discourses, this space was constantly reversed and shifted by their nurturing reproductive desires. The identities of these women were an unfolding of becoming masculine, becoming feminine, becoming their fathers, becoming the quintessence, and a becoming of the third generation of feminism. These deterritorialized identities represent the multiplicities of these women. As their "identities becoming" passed through the middle of each of these strata, the "line of becoming" unfolded into leadership. "Identities becoming" examined how these women's identities sprang up from their "being." "Leadership becoming" segues the intimate unfolding of their identities into their perspectives on leadership in more detail.

# Chapter Five

# Leadership Becoming

The terms "leadership" and the closely related "management" are segmented in the masculine discursive voice. Thus in the hierarchical structure, the female voice is subservient to the male voice; masculine language overshadows the feminine. Deleuze and Guattari suggest that the question is not whether the status of women is "better or worse, but the type of organization from which that status results" (1987, p. 210). In place of an oppressive hierarchy, the emphasis here is on the contextual interaction between individuals and institutions.

In this section, the oppositions within leadership and power were deconstructed from the binaries within the data. As binaries were uncovered, they became deconstructed which "is a poststructural strategy for reading texts that unmasks the supposed 'truth' or meaning of text by undoing, reversing, and displacing taken-for-granted binary oppositions that structure texts (e.g., right over wrong, subject over object, reason over nature, men over women, speech over writing, and reality over appearance)" (Schwandt, 2001, p. 203-4). "Leadership becoming" is the unfolding between the masculine and feminine, power and powerlessness, authority and service, stereotype and difference, and resistance and adaptability. In this final section, I examined the binaries drawn, and then how the participants blurred them.

## UNFOLDING THE MASCULINE

Each participant was asked to define "leadership." The language of the deans and the associate deans exemplified a managerial, patriarchal discourse where the deans from male-dominated professions more frequently used words such as "outcomes," "achievement," and "success" to describe leadership, indicative of their environment. The dominance of masculine language corresponded with Foucault's "discursive formation," which he described as "homogeneous fields of enunciative regularities" (Foucault, 1972/2002, p. 117). As each participant defined "leadership," a repetitive pattern of managerial rhetoric resounded with only slight variation.

One dean described leadership as, "getting people to do what you think they need to do to help you accomplish your goals just because the goals are important, not because you're just in the business of getting people to do what you want them to do." This associate dean described leadership with language such as "productive," "business," "accomplishing," and "goals." Particularly for associate deans, leading was completing tasks, attending to details, and coercing others into the "business." Rather than leading, associate deans' orientation was more "managing." This associate dean from a female-dominated college illustrated the delineation between associate deans and deans with this comment:

*I'm not void of the visionary part but I don't find that of interest. And somebody like [the dean] really finds that of interest. And so we are nicely matched, because I love operations. I like her to say, okay, now we've got this situation. How are we gonna make it happen?*

Associate deans try to "make things happen" for their bosses while full deans have a different reality as the "face of the college." The associate deans function as managers in that they "monopolize all relevant knowledge within an organization," that includes a "sharp divide between 'thinking' and 'doing'" (McKinlay & Starkey, 2000, p. 111).

The full women deans' language was filled with a corporate discourse, but with a visionary motivational emphasis. Dean Dare defined leadership as getting "followers" excited about a certain direction, "motivated and willing to follow you through . . . towards that goal whatever that might be." Dean Dare was one of the full deans who recently transitioned from associate dean. Her language emphasized outcomes, goals, and engaging people but also motivation, a view that delineates the divide between the dean's mission to engage people, and the 'doing' of the associate deans. The deans desired to inspire others and the associate deans alluded to being a "role model." The deans, like the associate deans, still want to "make it happen," but they are interested in broadening people's views. Dean Emmett, a dean from a female-dominated college, used the phrase "larger than the self" to describe her leadership role for expansion of faculty perspective within the organizational discourse.

*Well leadership is helping people see a big picture and seeing that they can become part of something larger than the self because if you only focus on the self, and one of the problems I think about leadership and higher ed. is that when you*

*work with faculty it's an intensely narcissistic profession, because (. . .) you're*
*always focused on the self. And leadership is about how do you break down that*
*wall and get faculty to commit to something larger than the self.*

Inherent in "leadership" is the existence of followers, and Dean Dare said,
"you can't have a leader without followers." All the participants started as
academics and segued into leadership; they understand how faculty are rewarded and the difficulty of expanding faculty's perceptions of their role in
the institution. There is intense competition for resources between faculty that
negates the focus on "something larger than the self." Another dean stated that
"no individual can be successful on their own." Even these female-dominated
college deans utilized masculine metaphors such as "breaking down the wall."
Still the goal of this dean was to persuade faculty to follow the goals of the
dean or institution. The five full deans described motivating and inspiring
others to "see a big picture" and move in that direction. These deans added a
visionary dimension of leadership to the pragmatic organizational language
that echoed the leadership literature in that discourse. Warren Bennis distinguished leaders using language such as "challenge," "conquer the context,"
"eye on the horizon," and "do the right things," which portrays a pragmatic,
visionary discourse (cited in Carter-Scott, 1994, p. 12).

Although their language paralleled the leadership literature discourse, these
women did not understand formally delineated leadership styles or cite leadership literature. Associate Dean Bennett reported attending a summer leadership course, but stated this:

*I've never studied (leadership styles) so it's just comes to me. (laughs) You*
*know? (laughs). So I think it's one of those things that's in your gut that you*
*have it to do to do a leadership kind of job. [. . .]. You know, leading could be,*
*here's the task, you do it and you do it in this way.*

Although she had not studied leadership, she described leadership as something innate. In retrospect, Dean Bennett understood that tasks are to be done
in a certain way but was ambiguous about whether this is leadership. She
spoke of leadership as completing tasks, but later in response to "what made
you a leader," she reported that she "bristled at the term leader." While these
women's language reflected the masculine, hierarchical discourse, the term
"leadership" was loaded in the emotional context of experience as demonstrated by Dean Bennett. What unfolded in the text was discomfort with the
masculine discourse.

Among the health-related professions, participants described the hierarchy.
In this example, the masculine colleges, deemed supreme over the feminine
colleges, shows the pervasiveness of these patterns.

*. . . the accepted hierarchy there is medicine is the big dog, dentistry is the next one and then there's everybody else. (. . .) But I really think it's always medicine, dentistry, poor nursing is always dead last, and nobody knows what to think of public health and health professions, you know, they're emerging as a concept. (laughter)*

This dean later pointed out that this hierarchical structure is equated with salary; those with the highest salaries have the most prestige. Later, the dean pondered on how these concepts affected her daughter as well as all women. These deans reflected on how their roles translated to the next generation of women. Although these women used rhetorical language when defining leadership, as the interviews continued, each woman's viewpoint became increasingly multidimensional.

## UNFOLDING THE FEMININE

Whatever the understanding of gender roles in leadership, most feminist perspectives launch into an "oppositional discourse of masculine versus feminine leadership," in which masculine leadership is presented as "competitive, hierarchical, rational, unemotional, analytic, strategic and controlling, and feminine leadership as cooperative, team working, intuitive/rational, focused on high performance, empathetic and collaborative" (Loden, 1985, cited in Court, 2005, p. 4-5). The masculine discursive voice was evident in the participants' language defining leadership. However, the vertical hierarchy of the leadership language unfolded subtle feminine characteristics that were horizontal, or collaborative, in nature. A masculine view of collaboration is that it undermines one's power thus creating weakness (Brunner, 2005). One associate dean confirmed that her collaborative leadership style was seen as weakness because she seldom made a decision "without talking to other people;" a trait seen as indecisiveness to her superiors. There was evidence that collaboration in a hierarchical structure does not lead to powerful positions; however, there was contradictory language as well.

Although the deans used a hierarchical discourse when defining leadership, the definitions revealed elements of collaboration and service.

*But leadership is really about, it's, it's about success. (. . .) You know, we all, take from one another, we gain strength from one another, [. . .] and, that's what I have always believed was my greatest strength is helping other people to, to reach their potential.*

First, Dean Vitalia equated leadership with success, a position at the top of the hierarchy, but then emphasized the necessity for individuals to gain strength from each other. This expands Dean Emmett's "larger than the self" text where faculty need to focus outside themselves, but then connects individuals to each other, not only committing to the institution. The deans' language emphasized motivation and inspiration of others and helping "followers" reach their potential is their service.

The discourse of collaboration lends readily to one of service. Service connects individuals to each other, and leadership has an element of fulfilling needs in others. Women historically participated as deans in student affairs to first serve women students, and later accepted this expanded role to serve male students (Nidiffer & Bashaw, 2001). These "service" positions were deemed appropriate roles which aided the ascension of women into higher education administration during the beginning of the twentieth century. Dean Sasser, from a male-dominated college, illustrated this concept by saying, "a lot of times leadership is somebody stepping up to the plate [. . .] seeing a need and filling it- being willing to say, 'yes,' a lot of people say, 'no.'" These women often ascended to their positions because they were willing to perform duties that their male peers did not want to do; these women said "yes" instead of "no." This discourse of service was especially present in the language of the women from the male-dominated colleges. Dean Dare illustrated this:

> *I've only been a dean for 2 1/2 years. I was associate dean for seven years and that's truly a service. . . . Because as an associate dean, I mean I really felt more like a servant of the college in the sense that, . . . my job was to make sure I was assisting education and make sure that you know everything ran right, everything was fair and appropriate, and I suppose I had power in the sense that we would judge student cases, and I did have the power to admit and dismiss students and I suppose those are powerful things, but they were really just the business of the college.*

The "business of the college" is what associate deans do; however, fulfilling needs is part of the college business. Dean Dare's attitudes about service helped propel her into the deanship.

One element of deconstruction includes a constant "self-revising, self-correcting, continual reaffirmation of itself, taking responsibility from moment to moment for itself, if it is to have a self, a 'yes' followed by a 'yes' and then again another 'yes'" (Caputo, 1997, p. 200). These assistant deans also constantly look outside of themselves and "say yes" to the needs of students and faculty; however, this attitude stays within the boundaries of the university's goals. Historically, women leaders have been known for their ability to create collaboration and build consensus in organizations (Brunner, 2005). These women deans motivate others, but also their ability to inspire motivated them-selves. Inspiration and motivation adheres the institution together to achieve its mission, and the deans' language is immersed with this discourse. Dean Langer, a dean in a female-dominated college, illustrated this by saying,

> *I really think that leadership, involves being able to inspire other people. (. . .)*
> *You know, paint the picture, make people excited about it- get them to say, wow!*
> *You know, that would be neat.*

This leader inspired people to think differently about the corporate strategy and to "make it happen," but used unique language such as "paint the pic-ture" to inspire others. Consensus, cooperation, and collaboration are all the watchwords of participatory management, terms frequently used in corpo-rate discourse; however, this language is secondary to hierarchical discourse. Leadership is primarily a vertical framework and supercedes the horizontal adhesive that holds "followers" together.

Dean Highe spoke of the importance of a "diverse faculty, diverse student body" that she admitted was harder to do in "this environment," alluding to an environment that was the antithesis of a horizontal collaborative repre-sentation. "Shared governance" and "ownership" are terms these deans used; however, they were blurred in a predominately vertical environment where accountability and surveillance exist.

Although these deans emphasized collaboration, the deans acknowledged that they have techniques to move their agenda by selling their ideas to a few before taking them to the whole.

> *If you want a decision to go your way, (. . .) best thing to do is you go and you*
> *start, you have a conversation, with a couple of people and you see where they*
> *are and you know you may tweak your ideas a little bit and you see oh, I really*
> *think this would be really good for us so, they start talking about it (. . .), then*
> *you already have a cadre of people that are on board. (. . .) Then you know sell*
> *it, in effect to their . . . colleagues.*

In this way the deans "massaged" their agenda. The deans used the conver-sations to gauge the success of their venture, but also directed what they deemed as important to the college. This was a method by which the deans directed all relevant knowledge within an organization (McKinlay & Star-key, 2000). Although the deans all talked about collaboration, the deans use their position to direct decisions. The deans shared their ideas to employ-ees prior to implementation to insure success. Although there may be times where these conversations consider employees' input, many employees are wary to disagree with supervisors. This is a deliberate way of producing consensus to direct knowledge.

Dean Emmett discussed this theme of consensus.

*You want to share it. And also when you have power you're also thinking about how to distribute it, so that other people have it. So that, and then you give them the freedom to make their decisions,(. . .) I say look, if you make mistakes that's okay. I mean, I don't mind if people make mistakes because that's a learning experience. I only mind when you make the same mistake twice.*

Dean Emmett wants to share power to create ownership and consensus to move her agenda. Freedom is given when people "work with" this dean, but the dean also determines what qualifies as mistakes. There is a tension between the "gift" of freedom in decision-making and making mistakes. In this context, decision-making is not empowerment, but is still harnessed by the dean. The deans determine and shape what is knowledge and power.

The dean controls the "regime of truth" for the college (Foucault, 1984, p. 74). Dean Emmett, a dean from a female-dominated college, spoke of being careful yet being transparent when using power, because other people "know perfectly well you have it.;" although there was a contradictory message in being just so transparent to achieve trust, yet keeping some things hidden. Power resides in the leaders' actions yet also in the leader's discretion to conceal or be transparent. In certain personnel matters, administrators cannot reveal details thus keeping relevant information shrouded and rumors escalating. Controlled meanings can transform into chaos and destabilize the organization. The deans' success may be determined by how well some truth is veiled and managed. Because of these factors, shared governance is difficult since there are many things that must remain hidden.

How the dean portrays truth affects the power of her college. Although the feminine side of leadership exemplifies collaboration, the deans are the top of the hierarchy and direct what knowledge is deemed important and correct. Where the intersection lies between the vertical hierarchy and the horizontal collaboration of an institution determines the culture of that institution. In deconstruction, both the masculine and feminine binaries are needed for the institution to exist; neither form is altogether absolute. The intersection of the stratified vertical and horizontal nature of leadership can be blurred by things hidden. This blurring functions as a fold which avoids the simplistic reversal of binaries and seeks the middle (Badiou, 1994). Although the participant's language can be distinguished into binaries, contradictions and discrepancies in the text collapse into deconstructive multi-dimensional concepts.

## POWER

Power in western culture has been conceptualized as "dominance, control, authority, and influence over others and things" (Brunner, 2005, p. 126). The "power-over" concept has been heavily researched and analyzed by Etzioni (1961) as coercive, remunerative, and normative (prestige) power, and delineated by French and Raven (1959) as reward, coercive, legitimate, referent, and expert power. Within the concept of "power-over" is the notion of its opposite-- powerlessness (Brunner, 2005). In a 1998 study, Brunner and Schumaker found that men tended to use power to achieve their own view of a community's common good rather than using their position to pursue the collective common good. The "power-over" concept is thought to be masculine while "power-with" is considered a feminine characteristic. Women tend to generate power by empowering others and creating change via their roles as mothers and teachers (Miller, 1993). However, this feminine power still has a directional pull as women function in a nurturing role, caring for those subordinate to them.

The nature of power in poststructuralism is described using different language and strategies. For Foucault,

> Power must be analyzed as something that circulates, (. . .). It is never localized here or there, never in anybody's hands, never appropriated as a commodity or piece of wealth. Power is employed and exercised through a net-like organization. And not only do individuals circulate between its threads; they are always  in the position of simultaneously undergoing and exercising this power. They are not only its inert or consenting target; they are always also the elements of its articulation. In other words, individuals are the vehicles of power, not its points of application. (Foucault, 1976, p. 98).

Individuals do not hold power, but power resides within an organization of relationships within a discourse. Foucault used the term "discourse" as an inclusionary/exclusionary system to help us understand how we are positioned as subjects which creates our relative power in each discourse. There are rules within a discourse concerning who can make statements and in what context, and these rules "exclude some and include others" (Craib, 1992, p.186). Differences in discourse spark conflict, and feminist studies assert that all people have the capacity to resist oppression (Weiler, 2003). Foucault thought that although the subject is affected by knowledge and power, it is "irreducible to these," so the "subject actually functions as a pocket of resistance to established forms of power/knowledge" (Alvesson & Skoldberg, 2001, p. 230). Power is passed back and forth from leader/subject and male/female depending on the context.

While power in the Western tradition differentiates readily into binaries, post-structuralism focuses on the circular nature of power. In the next section, I analyzed responses pertaining to questions about the production and negotiation of power, concentrating on power's revolving relationship between constituents.

## UNFOLDING POWER

Power and leadership are closely connected in these leaders' speech as power produces knowledge (Foucault, 1977/1980). As Foucault suggests, "power has to be analyzed in terms of relations of power" (p. 208). When asked how they produce power, most participants immediately transitioned into a traditional leadership discourse.

> *I use power . . . to build enterprises to build programs of excellence to motivate people, // to let them take their passion to the next level //with a strategic agenda, so // that's how I use it. I sorta set out the vision and give people the opportunity to execute it.*

Dunlap's text began with an ambiguous "I don't know," but then immediately segued into rhetoric such as "build," "passion," "vision," "execute" and "programs of excellence." Her words reflected the goals of the university in the hierarchical discourse of leadership. Leadership and power reflect each other in the text.

Dean Dare described power as the ability to make decisions that are measurable through resource allocation. Dean Dare's response to negotiating power seemed enigmatic at first, but then she quickly transitioned into how power is manifested in these concrete terms.

> *I think a lot of power comes from your personal connections from other powerful people, and I've been, impressed by that. Impressed by how, // how positive interpersonal relationships with say the president or the provost or the vice president actually gets you stuff. (laughter) (. . .) And I guess that stuff is what you might call power. (. . .) But you know I still believe deans are middle management in this environment. . . .*

 Dean Dare stated that power is derived from connections with other powerful people who are in the hierarchy above the deans. Dean Dare presented the importance of developing relationships with those above her to "get you stuff." Employees frequently lack awareness of those relationships above their direct supervisors, and Dean Dare was cognizant of her status in the hierarchy and considered her position middle management. Dean Dare's husband advised her; "job one is keep your bosses happy." "Brokering power" was a learned skill for this dean. Most women have difficulty culturally in self-promoting, but Dean Dare learned this skill in order to "serve" the college. The deans gain power by "managing up" as well as "managing down." Keeping your boss happy is expected for her and by her, and that attitude becomes the expectation for the college. "Stuff" is concrete evidence of power allocation throughout the university whether it is new hires, equipment, or buildings. The full deans mentioned buildings and upgrades to their physical plants during their tenure as evidence of their productive power. Dean Highe echoed this theme, but described how she gives power through providing budgets to department chairs to "give them power to make a difference in their environment." The budget is a source of power, but money is often allocated by the utilization from the prior year, which diminishes the "gift" of power by the deans.

The deans described delegating decision-making, but the deans only delegate those opportunities in situations that they deem appropriate.

*Everybody doesn't get to share in every decision. There are certain things that are my decisions. I know the most about them, I should make them. ( . . .) If they're recommending something that doesn't make sense because they don't' understand it, then I have to assume I didn't do a very good job of explaining it well. . . . I think you distribute that power in a very deliberate way. It doesn't happen accidentally.*

Dean Langer previously had described her consensus-building leadership style as something she was proud of, but she distributed power deliberately and not everybody gets to share in all decisions because she has the knowledge base and the decisions are hers. Dean Langer took responsibility if the faculty made a recommendation that contradicted her reality, and articulated how issues are explained to control the establishment of truth. Her reality monopolizes all relevant knowledge within an organization (McKinlay & Starkey, 2000). Although this corporate discourse was pervasive throughout the text, the deans also added language that reflected different forms of power.

Highe had been a dean for over ten years in a male-dominated college, and she described power being created through diversity. In this case, power was not just institutional but also multidimensional.

*Leadership to me is, having a sense of direction and bringing people together to help move in that direction. . . . that there are different ways to achieve those goals and ( . . .) to help make sure there is enough diversity in methods of achievement which means different kinds of people to be involved in the whole process so that you can really use the power of everybody you have to move an enterprise forward if it's big enough.*

Although Dean Highe was in a masculine-dominated college, her text emphasized "difference" and "diversity" that resonates with the discourse of the
third wave of feminism. This practice is consistent with the poststructural focus of Kristeva on diversity of identification, where rather than focusing on
the hierarchies of male versus female, the goal is to internalize the rivalries
of the difference thus celebrating the individualism of each person's identity
that "patches together a diversity of ethnic, regional, sexual, professional,
and political identifications" (McAfee, 2004, p. 102). She encouraged difference which in turn is "using the power of everybody" to exemplify expanding
boundaries and broadening views.

"Bringing people together" implied the concept of shared governance. One
dean from a female-dominated college stated that the power was not hers, but
because of shared governance "the power belongs to this college . . . , and
this college has become more powerful." She believed that creating shared
governance gave her college more power in the vertical framework of the
university. Several deans reiterated that the power belonged to the institution,
and their job was to support the institution. Although diversity and shared
governance may enhance the level of power, the institution still owns it, not
the faculty or the dean. There is a circular expansion/contraction and inclu-
sion/exclusion of power that exists within this organization.

On the other hand, several women discussed their lack of power in their
college. The associate deans described their supportive role and understood
that their power came from their position and proximity to the dean. One
associate dean reported that she did not have "much power in the organization, except what people give to me in their own brains. . . . It is only when
I am standing in for the dean that I then have the power of her chair behind
some of these interactions in which I engage." This is reminiscent of the Foucaultian view that 'truth' and 'knowledge' are socially constructed products
of interests and power relations (Hines, 1988). This same associate dean in a
female-dominated college told a story about how her lunch group was called
the "power lunch" by faculty. This informal lunch group was made up of past
administrators who rarely discussed work; however, she attributed power
given to this group as "fantasies about what goes on behind closed doors."
Her description showed the illusive nature of power, and that power given to
others may not be reality in their view. Knowledge that appears to be hidden
becomes powerful, and the powerless become powerful.

## UNFOLDING POWERLESSNESS

The five full deans used words such as "motivating" and "inspiring" to define how to produce power in others. The five full deans readily answered

this question because they must delegate. The associate deans for the most part, did not even address producing power except for Dean Wilson, an associate dean from a female-dominated college. Initially, she stated that "the term 'produce power' just doesn't ring a bell for me." Later, she reported that power was "building consensus," but had never reflected about creating power. Associate Dean Wilson had been an integral part of college operations for over twenty years, and her current dean had described their college as "powerless" and "often discounted as . . . not a real academic discipline." While Dean Wilson personally had difficulty with the term "produce power," her response illustrated how women leaders wield power in context to her experience with a former dean.

> *(This present dean) if anything, she's goes the other side of keeping people informed and in the loop. (. . .) . . . (The previous dean) just did it. And (this dean's) very much not like that. (. . .) I'm in the loop, I have knowledge, I understand where we're headed, and those things make me feel more confident, and therefore, in terms of knowledge, power, and in terms of association, power, and so on. Then I do have, and I do feel that I have more power, now than I did with a different boss. (. . .), because (the previous dean) went to the things she considered to be important. (The current dean) does more delegation of that kind of thing, so more of us have had that experience.*

The previous dean did not communicate her knowledge about college business, thus creating a sense of powerlessness implying that communication creates power. Dean Wilson further claimed that the college had more power with the new dean's leadership. Dean Wilson discussed the production of power in context of her previous dean whom had hoarded power by not delegating or keeping her associate deans "in the loop." Delegation in this context was a part of producing power within the organization. The previous dean liked hoarding the important tasks, thus making little attempt to produce or give power.

Derrida deconstructs the idea of giving in relation to justice. A gift is something that cannot be reappropriated and "never appears as such and is never equal to gratitude" (Caputo, 1997, p. 18). If a person says thank you for a gift, the gift starts being destroyed; thus a gift is beyond the circle of gratitude. Gift-giving needs to go beyond calculation because there is a point where calculation must fail. A politics calculated "without justice and the gift, would be a terrible thing, and this is often the case" (Caputo, 1997, p. 19). Delegation is a leader's gift to employees; however, the paradox is that this gift is directed by the goals of the dean and the university. The failure resides where the deans want to "give" power, but control it as well. However, Dean Wilson appreciated the intent of her dean's delegation as she was immersed in the organizational discourse. The gift is impossible, yet possible in the circle of deconstruction.

## UNFOLDING AUTHORITY

Dean Vitalia spoke of giving people responsibility with authority, but then outlined that middle management faces the paradox of having responsibility with no authority.

> *Best way to produce power is to empower the people. (. . .) (laughter) Give them responsibility and authority to, now they, what is it, the definition of a co-ordinator is all the responsibility and none of the authority. (. . .) I don't think you really have power if (. . .) you want to be the only one with power, I guess that's authority.*

Dean Vitalia stated that the best way to produce power is to empower, yet if employees have no authority, then they do not lead but control. The tension in this paradox is that employees cannot be empowered without the freedom to own their power and vision. Dean Vitalia outlined that to have authority is to be the only one with power. Dean Highe summarized that producing power, "is to enable other people to achieve their goals that are consistent with the mission and goals of the college and university." Moving an enterprise utilizes the power of everybody, and Dean Highe recognized the need for diversity, a multiplicity of methods, but these goals must be consistent with the university. Enterprises and institutions are not democracies. Dean Highe reminded us that power is only given to accomplish the mission of the university and is not the people's power; thus the leader controls the rules of discourse. The dean's goal is to convince others that they own the vision when the organization actually does.

Dean Langer, who had one of the highest faculty satisfaction ratings in the university, tried to prepare employees, "to feel ownership of what the requirements are for the process . . . sense of greater ownership in the things that affect them." Her job was to persuade the faculty to buy into the institution's vision, but this creates an oppositional binary of resistance when faculty cannot align themselves to the institution. The "us" versus "them" power struggle is born. Dean Langer recognized the tension inherent in the term power.

> *I don't really like the notion of power. I like the notion of strength. Power to me tends to convey controlling other people. (. . .) I try not to use power. Although I'll bet you that people who see me as very powerful, (. . .) I think you, you know, if we want to try to cast power as something positive, (. . .) you know, I think that you use and produce maybe influence. I'm more comfortable with that word (laughs). By, . . . getting people engaged in processes. Getting them to feel that they can have ownership // of things. Perhaps initially starting out by rewarding or praising people for accomplishments, but eventually getting it so that it doesn't depend on me to reward it or to praise it.*

This dean liked the term "influence" instead of "power," to reframe this management of people's behavior. Dean Langer's power resided in convincing others that they have ownership and acknowledged that power comes from how others view her. In essence, her power was her employees' gift to her, not something she owned. This distinguishes the term "power" from "authority" which is something sought, not given. Still the text exemplified the dean's need to mold her faculty into a cohesive unit through praise and reward. In her reality, there is a difference between "power" and "strength" which is distinguished by the presence or absence of control. Here, there was a blurring of definitions where these terms so closely resemble each other, but connote an entirely different meaning to the speaker according to that person's experience.

Associate Dean Sasser, like Dean Langer, did not like the term "power," but preferred the word "influence."

> *Because power outside, I mean, and the energy can't, I can't control somebody else. (. . .) And that's been a hard lesson for me to learn because I'm really like, controlling (. . .) And it's been a hard lesson for me to recognize that I could have influence on other people and I really don't have power over them, but I obviously I do have power over the students here, so there are some ways I do have power here. And in that way I guess I try to exercise that power in a caring manner, rather than an absolute power . . . .*

Dean Sasser equated power with control, and was very uncomfortable with the idea of power over others. Dean Sasser desired a "nurturing" power that revealed her reproductive values. Perhaps one reason Dean Sasser was unable to ascend further into administration because she controls instead of leads. Her power over students may be because she serves them well in that position of authority. However, the focal point is that although the women leaders equated power with control, they disliked that concept. They try to create "ownership" and shared governance which is discursive language for control. For Foucault, "relations of force and power are involved at every level of a discursive formation" (Macey, 2000, p. 101). However, these women know that there are tensions between what they do and who they are.

Empowerment is not the same as Derrida's "gift" because the people are only empowered if their goals coincide with administration's goals, which was then reframed as "ownership." Control cannot give power as leadership can. The gift of leadership is only given when there is not control, and thus the deans are uncomfortable with using authority to move their agendas. These deans repeatedly described this struggle created by leadership. In this example, Dean Sasser was torn by her ambition and the power she wielded.

*Contrast legitimate power to personal power*

*I am driven by power and I don't like to think about that. (. . .) You have to have power in a leadership position. (. . .) . . . did Gandhi have power? Did Mother Theresa have power? Yet they were great leaders. (. . .) But they had power in some way. So I think you've got to have power in order (. . .) to be truly effective. (. . .) I hope I use power compassionately,(. . .) more to meet a greater need and to serve others.*

Dean Sasser's position was what Hershey, Blanchard, and Johnson (2001) would call "legitimate" power, yet by her dialogue, she sought Gandhi's and Mother Theresa's personal power, individuals with the charisma, political skills, energy, and ability to articulate a vision that is independent of other sources of power (Hershey, Blanchard, and Johnson, 2001). However, both Mother Teresa and Gandhi exemplified power that was devoted to service. Certainly her dialogue reflected Greenleaf's (1979) "servant leader" kind of power as the kind of leader she desired to be. Dean Sasser was torn by the contradictions inherent in her role as a leader in a male-dominated college, and her own personal values reflecting her feminine reproductive desires.

Her perspective concurs with Brunner and Schumaker's (1998) study where men tended to use power to achieve their own view of a community's common good rather than using their position to pursue the collective common good. However, this study illuminated the amount of internal conflict women have when using power. These women disliked the masculine "power-over" control concept while emulating the "power-with" feminine characteristic. These women wanted to generate power by empowering others and creating change via their reproductive roles.

Dean Dare also shared some of Dean Sasser's conflicts about power.

*. . . power scares me to some extent because I know that I do have power in terms of hiring decisions, firing decisions, resource allocation. But I try to have a healthy respect for that and almost a fear (chuckle) of that power to make sure that it's used properly to advance the organization or know that we're doing something good for the profession or for the college and so I try to treat it, you know, with healthy respect . . . and not with, you know, abandon or . . . you know I think it's very easy to misuse power and so I try to . . . really be thoughtful about how you use it.*

Dean Dare described the judicious use of power with healthy respect so to adhere to the goals of the organization. Her thoughtful dialogue reflected her reproductive values of "doing good" but also her caution to not "misuse power," by using words such as "fear," "respect," and "thoughtful." These women described the "mantle of authority" -- being careful how they use their words and the power it implies. These deans cannot speak "off the cuff" in their professional life. Dean Sasser said her language became "amplified" and "took on a life of its own," and as a result, she learned to recognize the extent of her power. However, Associate Dean Sasser, while earlier stating that she was "driven by power," later suggested that power was given to her by her position and not sought by her. As Foucault reminds us, "power must be analyzed as something that circulates, (. . .) and not only do individuals circulate between its threads; they are always in the position of simultaneously undergoing and exercising this power" (Foucault, 1976, p. 98). These women used power, and were acted on by power. Power is circular and multidimensional.

## UNFOLDING SERVICE

I started reviewing and correcting the text of the deans from male-dominated (MD) colleges and then of the deans from female-dominated (FD) colleges. I noticed that I got progressively more melancholy while working on the female-dominated deans' text. As I explored my own subjectivity in this process, I perceived the language of the MD deans emphasized "service" to students and the university while the FD deans focused on gaining power and authority. To understand my reaction, I examined the text of Dr. Dunlap, who had recently undergone a cataclysmic experience with the leadership in her college. For years she had been extremely successful in her predominately female profession and now had moved into another arena with all-male colleagues. Her text illustrated her dilemma.

*Whereas the department chairs are // led and incentivized by different agendas that's not consistent with this and I'm not in a position of power to set the agenda and direct it. (. . .) (chuckle, sigh) I've been a total failure// in trying to get the department chairs to buy into this vision and to be a partner in it. It has been a very hostile environment.*

Recently, Dr. Dunlap had been pulled into what she called a "witch hunt." For over three hours they, "called me every jerk that you can name, everything that I value and everything that I am proud that I am, was raped." There had been a established college culture, and Dr. Dunlap came with her own resources, agenda and vision of how the university could become "world class." In her perspective her male colleagues were going to "build their empire" without concern of the "broader common good" but for "their reflective glory." Through this process, she had learned to have a "tough skin." This text illustrated her process of the reflective reframing of her experience.

*You know we lose sight of the fact, great leaders, // remember that they are stewards of resources, they are stewards of talent and the commitment is to the*

*community. (. . .) If you count what this enterprise is here and what we're do-*
*ing, that is success. (. . .) But was it really success // in other people's eyes, of*
*course not, because it wasn't about them or it wasn't about their agenda. (. . .)*
*It was never about me. Great leaders are never about themselves.*

Dunlap stated that successful leadership is not about the leader but the
mission of the community. The success was not hers, but the enterprise. She
survived by focusing on being a steward and her service to the community.
Another element was her "failure" to convince her colleagues to "buy into"
her agenda. Because of her contribution of resources, she expected this environment to conform to her vision. The process of "folding, unfolding, refolding" (Deleuze, 1988/1993, p. 137) was difficult in the emotional context of
her story. She inferred that she was a great leader because her agenda was the
"correct" one. While leadership is about holding onto values in the face of
opposition, the dichotomy was certain and in this case, formidable.

The outcome of this conflict was moving her and her resources to another
area of the university. Dunlap understood that the university wanted programs
of excellence, yet stated, "I'm bringing lots of money to the university. . . .
If it were about me, they would have locked me in that room and thrown the
key away." The money keeps her in her organization, not only her commitment to excellence. In another text she stated that, "using power to intimidate
people or using power to manipulate people or using power to just make more
money is short lived." Elsewhere she talked about the resources she brought
to the institution: "that is success if you can count the numbers." These contradictory statements represent her process of reframing the context. During
her crisis, the text illustrated the extremes of thinking she experienced. In her
process of "becoming," she was "not defined by points that it connects, or by
points that compose it; . . . it passes between points, it comes up through the
middle" (Deleuze and Guattari, 1987, p. 293). During this vulnerable period,
Dr. Dunlap was undergoing her own deconstruction of herself as she went
through the process of unfolding and refolding.

In this next statement, Dunlap speaks of the contradictions of success.

*. . . you know success can be toxic, you know. (. . .) But good things happen*
*and you lose sight of the balance in life that you need to be in the moment. °You*
*need to stop and be in the moment° //(. . .) if you don't take time to (. . .) . . .*
*well, to rejuvenate your own soul, you can't be effective for all the people who*
*are counting on you.*

In times of conflict, people reframe the text in order to survive. Dunlap has
been very successful in the hierarchy, yet speaks of the toxicity of success.
The binaries between good and bad are balanced by reflective middle. Her

dimensions of life expanded and contracted as she sorted her thoughts. Several times she referred to herself as the "Eveready Bunny" who has been able to fulfill expectations and "make it happen." However, she found that by not keeping in contact with herself and her family in recent years, she "hit the wall" and now the "Eveready Bunny" has been "sent down a different path." She survived a catastrophic event because she reframed the circumstances to fit her values—service for the community.

Through this process, Dr. Dunlap transformed her sense of self and was not destroyed. Perhaps her perspective on "empire-building" and the "greater good" was only her reality. However, her story illustrates how for some women, a mission of self-preservation does not protect them in times of crisis. Individuals get washed away and destroyed as their sense of self disappears. Dr. Dunlap's values of service kept her focused in the midst of the crisis to help "rejuvenate her soul." My subjective reading of the text unfolded these contradictory statements as her reframing process transformed this adversity into a reality she could live with. During difficult times, this process is necessary to rejuvenate and renew the soul.

Her previous college may have not been "wrong" or "evil," but may have not recognized her agenda as complementary to their discourse. She was the "outsider" coming in and disrupting the status quo. On the other hand, women who enact the masculine conceptions of power make others very uncomfortable around them (Brunner, 2005). Dr. Dunlap recognized on some level that "gender bending" was occurring by pondering, "Am I some self-aggrandizing bitch or am I really here to do something great or good?" She had stated elsewhere in the text that she knew she had been called a "bitch" behind her back. Brunner reported that women who did not hold to feminine conceptions of power, were not liked, were considered unsuccessful, were not labeled as 'powerful,' and were called 'bitches" (2005, p. 134). Dr. Dunlap understood that she 'failed" to influence the college's agenda; on the other hand, she envisioned her continued success in another realm of the university.

After reading this interview transcript, I reflected on my dislike of the texts of the participants from the female-dominated colleges, and sensed an aura of inadequacy that permeated the texts. The female-dominated deans seem to be "empire-building" as they attempted to hoard their power. As I looked at the text of the female-dominated deans, I perceived a pervasive need for power which translated into a sense of insecurity that I did not perceive in the male-dominated deans. Here is an example from one interviewee.

*. . . to be a good leader, (. . .), you have to understand that you have power and you have to be not afraid to use it. (. . .) Because if you act as if you don't have it, (. . .) you aren't going to be effective, because it's inherent in your role. // I have a lot of power.*

This participant singularly stated that she had "a lot of power." Other interviewees who had been in their positions for many years never described themselves in this way. Her interview was filled with nuances of control. Unlike
other participants who used their power cautiously, this interviewee declared
that to be cautious with power makes you ineffective. My subjective reading
of the text interpreted a sense of insecurity because people who say they have
power often do not.

Another interviewee from a female-dominated college liked having the opportunity to select new hires because it was "very powerful." Later in another
section, she reported that she liked working with other people around campus because of her position, and "they would take my call because they knew
who I was; it's a power position, but I call it fun--clearly its power." This interviewee liked the power gained from her role as an administrator. Certainly
connections with other powerful people gain power, but this rhetoric was less
apparent with male-dominated deans whose discourse centered on service.

In another interview, a participant disparagingly said that in her female-
dominated college the "focus is that everybody should feel good." Her
response to one student was, "I'm sorry, sometimes, you can't feel good
about what you wrote because what you wrote was crap, and it needs to
get better." She also complained that her college suffered from "intellectual flabbiness." Her degradation of her college was evident throughout her
interview, and a recurrent theme in the female-college interviews. Perhaps
these women in female-dominated colleges are "expressing 'outlaw emotions' such as envy and resentment that might be at odds with the caring
script" (Acker and Feuerverger, 1996, p. 402). Perhaps the female-dominated college deans and associate deans are compensating for not feeling
valued within the academy. The reasons were not clear as was my subjective understanding of these texts; however, a discourse of desire for power
and prestige was evident.

One dean was placed in a provisional program before being allowed into
a Ph.D. track in a top research institution because they said, "It's a little too
rigorous for you, dear." She reported that her profession had been historically "relatively powerless." An associate dean in a female-dominated college related, "I mean if somebody's going to give me a little power, I'll take
it. (laughter) (. . .) then I will use it, I hope, judiciously." All of these women
were extremely bright and articulate; however, the negative aura of being
from a female-dominated profession influenced their speech and attitudes
about their own professions. Attitudes of self-preservation resembled the
"empire-building" framework described by Dr. Dunlap. Their mission was
to seek power and self-preservation. Like Dr. Dunlap, these woman spoke of
acting "like men" in their careers. How these women stereotyped their inter-

actions with men and women unfolded more insights about how they negotiated power.

## UNFOLDING STEREOTYPES

In deconstruction the oppositional binaries are reduced to difference. Although the masculine supersedes the feminine in leadership, both masculine and feminine aspects are needed for the organization. Power is very present in the hierarchical structure of the institution, but the powerless can become powerful as diverse voices enter the landscape. In this section, the aspects of leadership and gender are viewed in the way that these women interact with others, male and female.

Power and gender are intimately related. Several of the women drew lines about how they are different than men then automatically transitioned into discussion about how power was used by both genders. Frequently they shared the perspectives of the first wave of feminism where women sought equal rights because they were "just like" men. One associate dean from a female-dominated college had a bumper sticker in her office that said, "Well-behaved women rarely make history" by Laurel Thatchers Ulrich (1976, p. 20). She admitted to not daring to put it on her car when she first came to her job and then brought up this story about power and gender.

*So power is an interesting thing. (. . .) when I first interviewed for an associate dean position at (a university) a very elderly "power man," not powerful, but loved power (. . .) asked, 'What would I do with the power that I had?' And I had to answer it three or four times, and he never accepted my answer . . . . But what was interesting is that he wasn't listening to me. (. . .) Now he never viewed the fact that I would be over him but in the hierarchy I was. And as it turned out other things happened and (. . .) he retired (. . .) and I still survived. (laughs)*

This associate dean identified this man who loved power, but also enjoyed her power over him. During these interviews, there was a lot of laughter when talking about men's behavior, and laughter when these women discussed "surviving" or "winning" in difficult situations. This associate dean believed that she was hired for that job because of her response to the "power man" and was exuberant that she "survived." This suggests an inherent fear of not surviving which was pervasive in the participants' voices. She then reiterated the fact that women are under more scrutiny compared to male colleagues.

*The men that I have worked with have never acknowledged that they don't know something. // They will take a job, they will take a promotion because of course they can do it. Well, they don't have to do it. They have women who will actually do it for them. Whereas women will say, I don't know. (. . .) Oh, yes. You have to see the people that I do. I think women are more reflective. They want to be successful. They know they're being observed. And their slightest failure becomes a big failure. A man's little failure is really not his . . . . (. . .) I see that men don't accept responsibility easily. (. . .) They rarely do the job- their job.*

The anger in the text is clear, with laughter directed at difficult interactions. This associate dean complained about the many incompetent men promoted and the subordinate women who do their work for them. This associate dean inferred that her female-dominated college promoted incompetent men. This gendered division of labor assumes that women will have primary responsibility for nurturing the young and serving men, but "receive little credit for doing so" (Acker & Feuerverger, 1996, p. 403). Another dean from a female-dominated college stated that male students respond in classes by saying, "whatever stupid thing that's in their head," and that "men out-talk women by a mile" despite what "everybody thinks." These women drew distinctions between men and women. Even in female-dominated colleges there was anger directed toward men who direct the conversation and therefore the discourse.

Although women in male-dominated colleges did not speak of their professions in derogatory terms, Dean Dare described the challenges of being in a male-dominated profession, and the responsibility she felt not to "mess it up" for other women.

*I think it's harder to be a leader in (. . .) my profession which is a very . . . you know it's a very male profession. (. . .) I've tried to always compensate by being twice as good and hoping to get half the credit, that's a cliché, but I think it's true. (chuckle) (. . .) I think that, you know, women are scrutinized more and critiqued more and the expectations are higher and it's just, // easier for, you know, something gets messed up for the guys to say, "See I told you so," kind of thing. So I think it just requires a level of competence that . . . you wouldn't necessarily expect of every male colleague.*

In this pseudo-soliloquy, she revealed her fear of scrutiny and her attempt to overcome that fear by being "twice as good." The fear of failure also stemmed from a sense of responsibility to succeed for other women coming behind her. The fear of failure existed in the text of both the female or male-dominated colleges; however, Dean Dare suspected that the "guys" wanted her to fail because "that's how it is."

*I think these guys, almost I sometimes think, would find joy in failure (chuckle) and so you have to ensure that that never happens and that's you know . . . I wouldn't call it a burden, but it's an important responsibility that you have to be aware of all the time. And I think the rules are different for women than for men and I (. . .) think everything you do, how you look, how you dress, how you behave, is always subject to scrutiny. And I'm not trying to paint an overly dramatic picture, but I think you just have to be honest about that and know that, "that's how it is."*

This dean perceived that every intimate detail is observed, and felt pressure to perform at a level that failure "never happens." This dean reported handling the tremendous pressure by being herself, preparation, acceptance of mistakes, and working through it every day, but always added a glint of humor when describing grim circumstances. The resilience and persistence was evident, and many women will not subject themselves to this level of scrutiny. These women feel the responsibility to not "mess up" for those women coming behind them. They do not just have pressure to perform their tasks, but the perception of intense scrutiny. However, these women do their job because it's who they are, and they have the strength to be who they are.

Women's characteristics were perceived in different ways by the participants. An associate dean in a male-dominated college explained that women are more compliant, and "they don't have a lot of power." She stated that she was speaking so liberally here because she was near the end of her career and had reached a point "where I don't care, I'm going to say what I'm going to say." She thought women were without power in this male-dominated college and were relegated primarily into non-tenured tracks. On the other hand, another interviewee perceived that women leaders seek consequences for mistakes where rather, "men make excuses for one another," and men are "buddies" who protect each other. Women do not necessarily protect each other and none of the participants specifically discussed mentoring other women for leadership. Dean Highe even told a story about an unpleasant experience working for a new woman administrator who reacted to Highe's self-confidence, deconstructing the stereotype that women are weak-willed and indecisive. Another dean described her experiences with working with women as well:

*Some women are tougher on women // than men are too. Of course that's an old syndrome. (. . .) Well some of it is because you know, 'by god, I had to suffer and you will too' // kind of model instead of mentoring and building capacity, . . . and some people are just punitive.*

This dean identified resentment as a reason why women do not like other women in leadership. The notion that women treat other women fairly is not accurate. Women do tend to compete with each other. Another dean specifically discussed the repercussions of firing two women whose spouses were on the faculty, and said, "I don't like not supporting women, but . . . they were decisions that needed to be made." Besides a few women colleagues, none of the deans or associate deans specifically mentioned helpful relationships with other women in leadership.

Although distinguishing gender roles in the data was evident, much of the text did not stereotype men in disparaging terms. These deans had learned these tools and skills from men, as these women had male mentors, not female. Few of these women mentioned their mothers influencing their career decisions or serving as role models in that respect. All of these women grew up in the seventies during the rebirth of feminism and acknowledged that because of their age most of their mentors were men. One dean from a male-dominated college declared, "I have not had women role models." These women relied on men as they ascended academia.

Even deans in female-dominated professions had male mentors. Dean Langer discussed that in her youth, her mentors were mostly women because of her profession; however, she later mentioned that as a dean her mentors became men.

*So my dad was an important person and then most of my mentors, teachers, people who encouraged me were women, teachers and women, really, peers. (. . .) Most of the men that I've had as mentors have come much later in my life, actually, since I've come to (this university). (. . .) And there have been some men who have been remarkably helpful and influential in my career. // But that didn't happen until well into it. (. . .)*

This dean mentioned how important her father was and suggested that he was her first mentor. While she has been proud of her career, she also perceived that being a dean of a female-dominated college was not a prestigious thing; she described the stereotypical dean in a female-dominated college as an "old, dowdy (. . .) dean of women." Rarely did the deans talk about other women leaders and those were primarily colleagues, not mentors. One dean from a female-dominated college, wanted to be in administration because she admired a male role model. So while drawing the lines between genders, these women blurred the boundaries by wanting to be like men. Dean Emmett and the deans from female-dominated areas often described themselves as "male-like."

*I have thought about this a lot, it creates a lot of conflict because even though I can work well with men, but, a lot of men resent me because I don't act like a woman. It's a very male style of leadership. Although you know I think that we should stop thinking about this as male and female and just say, this is this per-*

*son's style and don't worry about the gender piece attached to it. But I thought
a lot about it.*

Dean Emmett considered her disposition to be nurturing in her personal life
yet did not experience that in her professional life, and believed it was because of her male style of leadership. Again there is the thread of laughter
everywhere in the gender text. Another associate dean in a female-dominated
college described herself as "male in a female body," and said, "I have the
strength and the hutspa that often men have but I wear it differently." Although
this dean perceives her behavior as "male," she is careful to distinguish herself as different from men by saying, "I don't think I know everything." Later,
she demeaned her female-dominated college by saying, "And didn't quite understand why I was in a College of (X) anyway, but I figured, well, what the
heck!" Her bachelor's degree was not from that college in which she is now an
administrator, and in her interview she distanced her academic interests from
the undergraduate mission of her college. While these women distinguished
themselves from men, they also described themselves as men. By distinguishing the binary, these women become that which they stereotype.

The participants from female-dominated colleges described the need to
learn to "pay attention to other people's feelings." One interviewee stated "I
don't score real high in those affective areas of leadership," while the participants from the male-dominated colleges spoke of developing a "real thick
skin" so they "don't feel so much anymore." Perhaps those women in female-
dominated colleges face even higher expectations to manifest the "nurturing"
role or face conflict with female colleagues. Women are expected to be nurturing or be considered failures and face "chilly climate stories" (Acker &
Feuerverger, 1996, p. 409). These caretaking roles are not just expected by
men, but also by other women.

Another interviewee from a female-dominated college described herself as
masculine in behavior:

*And I'm gutsy enough, and I always lay the cards on the table. What's on my
mind I say; I'm not a manipulative person. (. . .) That's a very masculine trait.
People like Jack Welch [CEO of General Motors] did it all their lives, but women
who do it are considered bitches. (. . .) This is the way it is, it's . . . this is what I
don't agree with, this is what I agree with and I'm certainly wrong a lot of times,
but let's lay it on the table, let's discuss it and let's move forward. That's a very
masculine choice; it's not a feminine choice.*

The word "bitch" is not found in the literature written by men as a descriptive
term for women leaders, and is a term difficult to define. In one gender study,
when women leaders do not adhere to the feminine conceptions of power,

they are "viewed as unsuccessful (not well liked), disallowed the label 'powerful' by community members, and called 'bitches' by many participants during triangulation interviews" (Brunner, 2005, p. 134). This phenomenon was interpreted in this study as if these women were "gender bending- something extremely uncomfortable for others around them" (p. 134). These women are enacting their masculine conceptions of power, a role appropriate for their position in the discourse, but not for their own gender. In another study, women superintendents that acted like men and disrupted gender constructions, suffered "diminished access, poor support, personal attacks, unfair criticism, and short tenures" compared to other superintendents (p. 134-5). Dr. Dunlap experienced consequences for her masculine embodiment of power. Those "gender-benders" may face more difficulties because their masculine traits may stand out in female-dominated colleges. However, those same women may have been promoted because of their "male-like" qualities in the hierarchical masculine discourse. The "gender-bending" strategies are circular and cannot be segmented into simplistic binaries of social strata.

Being described in derogatory terms is difficult for anyone; however, women from female-dominated colleges often described themselves or profession in these derogatory terms. As previously mentioned, one dean described her college as suffering from "intellectual flabbiness." Another dean admitted that her female-dominated college was "powerless" and "discounted as not a real academic discipline" compared to the other colleges. These comments illustrated leaders who were not comfortable with what they represent and thus themselves. The real crux of these words lies in the knowledge that these deans become "that of which they speak" (Sarup, 1988, p. 70). These women place themselves in Adrienne Rich's "ontological basement" because a masculine ideology dominates the discourse from whence they came (Martin, 1985, p. 15). These women are not enamored with their feminine identities in their careers which are influenced predominately from their fathers and male mentors.

## UNFOLDING DIFFERENCE

In the previous section, those deans and associate deans delineated themselves from men or compared themselves to men; however, not all deans differentiated themselves through gender. Stereotypical absolutes were evident, but also revealed were the blurring of the masculine and feminine. Dean Highe seemed to have not reflected on how gender affected her leadership although she was in a male-dominated college. As we talked, she would mention the significance of gender only as an afterthought. When asked how being a woman changed her leadership, Dean Highe responded with this:

*You know it's hard for me to answer that because since I've never been a man, I don't know in those real ways. (. . .) One of the people I learned most about in terms of administering was a guy, (. . .) and, I really learned a lot from him, but . . . my personality was different from his. For example, he was more apt to probably be more abrupt in certain ways than I would be and, I would . . . listen a little bit longer (. . .) just to be sure I was fully understanding the between-the-lines elements of what I'm hearing and seeing and in an environment of what's the sort of emotional content, what's resonating against. (. . .) I don't know if that's because I'm a woman or not though. I know it's different from the way (the previous dean) behaved . . . it's different from the way (previous male president) behaved, different actually from the way (previous female provost) behaved.*

Dean Highe was reluctant to draw a line between what was male or female and blurred the gender line with this discussion. What she emphasized was difference in individual leadership. Dean Highe had not reflected on gender differences until this interview. Her previous mentor was male and she appreciated his contribution to her development but was not enticed to imitate his leadership style. However, Dean Highe chose to "resonate" to the emotional context of personalities- a more feminine approach, although not identified as one by her. Dean Highe pointed out that gender stereotypes did not fit leaders' behavior. Dean Wilson, a twenty-year veteran associate dean from a female-dominated college, ended her interview with this reflection:

*I was thinking again just about the whole gender issue and leadership or power. Sometimes I think that men and women do tend to have more gender related styles. And other times I don't think so at all. (laugh) Sometimes I think that the private versus the public sector had different leadership power, styles, and other times I don't think so at all. Sometimes people will say, "Well you know it's just because we're a bunch of women that we do- fill in the blank." And I look around me and some of the men I know are in positions of you know, fairly much authority and I think, "They do that too!" (laugh) (. . .) Sometimes I just think it's just very individual. °Very individual.° (. . .) And so there's some hesitancy sometimes (for women) to draw a line of expectations. But I don't find necessarily that men are very good at °drawing lines either.°*

Dean Wilson spoke with ambiguity about the leadership styles between men and women. She mentioned later in the text that men also do not like to fire and women leaders do not always show compassion for employees. Although several of the women were very vocal about differences between men and women, others were much more ambiguous about emphasizing differences. Although these genderized discourses shift between binaries, poststructuralism does outline the function of resistance in discourse. Differences in discourse inevitably spark conflict, and Foucault thought that although the subject is affected by discursive practices, the subject can resist "established forms of power/knowledge" (Alvesson & Skoldberg, 2001, p. 230). The next section specifically describes this negotiation of difference.

## UNFOLDING RESISTANCE THROUGH ADAPTABILITY

In the critical tradition, Freire believed that there are contradictions between the way the oppressed and the dominant culture perceives the world. Education reproduces existing gender inequalities, but feminist studies assert that all people have the capacity to resist oppression (Weiler, 2003). Freire thought resistance was necessary for the process of humanization as "we know how to resist so as to remain alive" (1998, p. 74). Freire described his own exile where he learned a resistance through adaptability that produced nonconformity by not giving up hope. While "resistance" and "adaptability" may seem to be opposing binaries, the deans' text illustrated the unfolding and refolding.

After Dean Dunlap revealed a recent confrontation with six male colleagues, she used the words "witch hunt" and "rape" to describe this shock to her identity. The entire interview recorded how her inner world negotiated this conflict. Her interview revealed that she had never thought about gender and leadership until this confrontation.

> But I never [thought] about my gender. They (. . .) misjudged me. They though I was a weak woman. They thought I would cry, they thought I would ball up and be emotional // and they attacked me. I . . . went home for 48 hours and did that. And I struggled with it, but (. . .) I didn't shrivel up and die. You know, when women respond, the first response is "Oh, she's just being emotional." I'm not being emotional, I'm being damn right. (Laughter)

Emotionalism has been equated with women as far back as Plato who described it as "womanish." Here Dunlap described emotion as weakness, but as she described her transformation, emotionalism became redefined as certainty. Because of this incident, she had to face her motives for her actions. In reflection, she decided that her motives were for the "greater good" and then expressed the feminine attributes of love and understanding toward her "attackers." Later in the interview, she reported that she "commanded the stage" for a national meeting with two of these "attackers" in the audience. She described that as a "moment of leadership." Although she was "over" being angry about the confrontation, she enjoyed her moment in the spotlight in the face of her attackers, the spotlight of resistance.

Most of the deans described difficult situations with men but not women, but were careful not to identify these as "female boss" versus "male employee" difficulties. Often the difficulties with male employees were detailed only when the tape recorder was turned off. In this example, one dean from a male-dominated college described a situation in which she had to promote someone she did not trust.

> *I have a lot of trust issues with and °I don't necessarily want to work with him.°*
> *(laughter) So, . . . I have this dilemma right now and (. . .) how do I (. . .) be true*
> *to my feelings and I feel, you know, as one of my basic requirements, I have to*
> *be able to trust people that work closely with me. (. . .) I personally have trust*
> *issues with you and if I'm going to give you this task, you need to tell me right*
> *now how we're going to work together and how I'm going to trust you and how*
> *I'm gonna, (. . .) I'm practicing this speech, . . . (laughter)*

In this soliloquy, Dean Dare reflected on how to negotiate this situation. Laughter reoccurred to lighten the mood as Dean Dare debated between being true to herself and the economic necessity of promoting someone she believed undermined her leadership. The paradox was the belief that she has to trust those she works closely with, yet her language exposed her lack of trust. Dean Dare suspected that this male faculty member did not respect her because of her gender, making this decision even more problematic. Her desire to work collaboratively was apparent, yet this text illustrated the difficulty she has neglecting her feelings. Collaboration is important to women (Brunner, 2005), and her inner conflict was demonstrated by her hardball speech. This example illustrated her perspective regarding how she interacts with men.

> *I think if I was 6' tall and silver gray hair, good looking guy, I think people*
> *(laugh) would either be more afraid of me or more automatically respectful.*
> *And I think . . . I think you have to earn it a little more, you know, if you're a*
> *(. . .) woman. You know, if you're a good looking guy, you've just got ahead start.*
> *But I walk fast (laughter) and I catch up . . . . (. . .) I mean I could not use that*
> *kind of imposing, // aggressive strategy to manage somebody that works for me*
> *or that I'm in charge of or need to get my . . . I have to get my point across in*
> *a much different manner because I'm not physically overbearing. (. . .) I would*
> *have, mentor students 6'4" and I'd say, "have a seat\" (laugh)*

Dean Dare perceived a power advantage of height, but used what strengths she has to her advantage. She negotiated power differently, but found methods that worked. "Have a seat" was a very powerful strategy that gives her control, but she also has to "walk fast, and catch up" to stay ahead in the hierarchy. Although leadership strategies do not encourage leaders to "tower over" employees and tell them off, men can do this successfully and rise to the top of the hierarchy. Dean Dare never used aggressive strategies to negotiate power because of unspoken social mores for women, and even joked about using a step stool to gain power. Studies have shown that women are considered successful when they behave like a 'lady,' a pattern of heteronormativity (Brunner, 2005). They must constantly adapt to the social mores to gain and maintain power. Certainly, Dean Dare understood where she stands . . . or cannot stand.

Collaboration in a hierarchical structure has been seen by men as weakness. However, collaboration is a paradox, collaboration can be powerful. Associate Dean Wilson from a female-dominated college described her current dean as someone who had gained much power for their college, and who was very collaborative compared to the previous dean.

> *I've been an administrator in this college with two deans, // who could not have been more different people. (the previous dean) (. . .) kind of relied on "the boys," meaning that cadre of men that I described earlier who were older, more traditional and so on to bail her and the college out in certain circumstances. . . . but her style of management and leadership is very different from (the current dean who) is much more . . . , if anything, she's goes the other side of keeping people informed and in the loop.*

This associate dean's reflection contrasts two ideologies of power. The current dean portrayed an image of success by keeping her women colleagues "in the loop" and delegating well to others in contrast to the other who rendered her subordinates powerless. The former dean would rely on her male colleagues to rescue her when she needed them, and they obliged but did not grant her or the college power. Although Dean Wilson stated that the previous dean could push her agenda effectively, she readily agreed that the current dean had vastly improved the physical conditions and the perceived power of the college that had traditionally been seen as "powerless." Dean Langer, the current dean, described her relationships with her male dean colleagues.

> *. . . And there's the guys. That's what I used to call them. Look, guys, you know. And they've been wonderful colleagues and at times I think I've been able to use humor to help them see, when they have perhaps been discounting something I said either because I was a woman or a (female professional). (. . .) Because I just haven't seen being a woman as standing in the way of what I wanted to do. Partly I guess, because if somebody had said to me my entire life, you can't do that. I've said, "watch me."*

This dean in a female-dominated college did not think being a woman was a disadvantage although she acknowledged that "the guys" would discount her at times because she was a woman in a female profession; however, there was no apparent anger in the text. She gained "the guys'" trust by working hard and being an "assertive communicator." She brought data to present her points but "never became, oh, my goodness, here comes that shrew to yell at us again." Dean Langer used humor and did not become embittered, and thus gained respect and power for her college. She empowered her employees through collaboration; however, with male colleagues, she negotiated with the male characteristics of assertiveness and logic. Humor was a tool of negotiation even in the face of being discounted. Her associate dean described the change in culture between the previous dean and the current dean.

> . . . but ten years ago, where I would be completely discounted // in a conversation, and I've felt like it was because I was a woman. // I was also younger, which the men tend to be older, so there could've been some reversed ageism (laugh) if you will there, // but at that point the guys were running that show.

Dean Langer played by the "guys'" rules; she brought data, was an assertive communicator, managed her anger, and thus gained power for her college. In the long run, her methods of gaining power for the college made a difference for her faculty and staff. While feminists may see her methods as acquiescing to the "guys," her methods are a form of resistance through adaptability. Dean Langer was in a female-dominated environment, but at the dean's level, she had to negotiate power with male colleagues and administrators. Dean Langer understood that she was discounted, but stated that being a woman never hindered her. In her interview, she reported losing some battles, but still won the war on a professional and personal level. She did not use men like the previous dean to "bail her out" and earned her male colleagues' respect over time. Dean Langer did not forsake her self-respect.

This dean had a father who supported her education and her identity. This link with the past helped her manage her relationships with her male "wonderful" colleagues, and thus lessen bitterness in her negotiations with them. In her younger years, her personal life reflected her competitiveness with her brother but always with a light-hearted humor that served as a training ground for her interactions with men. She would compete with him until he got stronger and then "figure out ways to be more cunning." Unfolding resistance through adaptability taught her how to negotiate power. This line of becoming connected her identity and her leadership and helped her pass through the middle of the binaries of the social strata. Avoiding the edges unfolded the process.

*Chapter Six*

# Conclusion

The oppositions within identity, leadership and power were deconstructed from binaries within the data. My interest focused on how these women constructed, "their subjectivitities within the limits and possibilities of the discourses and cultural practices that are available to them" (St. Pierre, 2000, p. 258). The identities of the participants shifted contextually within binaries of the social strata, "becoming" the identities of the masculine, feminine, father, third generation, and the quintessence. In "becoming" leaders these women unfolded within the masculine, the feminine, power, powerlessness, authority, service, stereotypes, difference, and finally between resistance and adaptability. The "lines of becoming" passed through these connecting points and created a multidimensional and multidirectional leadership persona.

The identities of these women as "leaders" were evident in their descriptions of themselves and were embedded in a masculine discursive voice. However, their descriptions also embodied the feminine and other characteristics not so easily segmented often interplaying within the masculine discourse. The texts explored these women's "practices of the self" (St. Pierre, 2005, p. 1) that considered the speaking subjects to determine their unconscious experiences in the social structure of educational leadership. Besides a few women colleagues, none of the deans or associate deans specifically mentioned being mentored by women or mentoring other women; they did not have female role models. These women's leadership identities, derived from their fathers whether positive or negative, sustained their interactions with men throughout their life, becoming the "identity of the father."

The language of the text was filled with a discourse of achievement and hierarchy; thus fulfilling the prophecy that a women who becomes an administrator is shaped or subjectified by the language of that discourse. Deleuze and Guattari suggest that the question is not about the status of women, but what type of organization "from which that status results" (1987, p. 210). The masculine identities of the deans helped them ascend this hierarchical environment; however, there was language blurring the masculine binary. While the deans were intent on success, they "loved" the diversity of responsibilities and the creativity in their positions.

Sometimes their feminine values were incongruent with the masculine discourse and created a source of conflict. This incongruence split their language and identities into labeled positive and negative traits where the masculine superceded the feminine. Perhaps being driven to create a "greater good" sanctioned their ambition; or an attitude of service quieted their productive desires so they could balance the productive and reproductive areas of their lives. Women can be both reproducers of the species and producers of culture, but the nurturing reproductive desires of women have historically motivated them for the "greater good." In a society where the masculine model of leadership permeates every institution, these women find ways to balance their lives.

Although these women used rhetorical language when defining leadership, as the interviews continued, without exception the text became increasingly multidimensional. Leadership was defined by these women as getting people to work toward the goals of the organization, but the term "leadership" was loaded with the emotional context of experience. Leadership for these women was something not learned from books, but something innate. Perhaps this is not surprising since most of the leadership literature echoes a masculine discourse which does not "resonate" with women. Leadership was not learned through courses and the mechanisms of society but resulted from the identities and intrinsic drives of these individuals. While the outside "folds us into identity" (St. Pierre, 2000, p. 260) and gave these women the discursive practices to ascend into leadership, their own constructions resulted in who they became as individuals. Deleuze and Guattari use these spaces together; "smooth space is constantly being translated, transversed into a striated space; striated space is constantly being reversed, returned into a smooth space" (1980/1987, p. 474). The outside and the inside identities of the participants folded and refolded.

The deans spoke of hierarchical vertical thinking, and then moderated those extremes with family and their interests. While research shows that women have difficulty balancing family and careers, these deans enjoyed and directed their busy lives, and were not unhappy about being preoccupied with work. Their lives were an extension of who they were as individuals, the quintessence or intrinsic constituent of their characters. Most of the deans did not come into leadership by their design or that of others, but had a vision of who they wanted to be and emerged into those positions. For these women, "being" came long before "doing;" and leadership was a "label" for their identities.

The vertical hierarchy of the leadership language had subtle feminine characteristics that were horizontal, or collaborative, in nature. Brunner and Schumaker found that men tended to use power to achieve their own view of a community's common good rather than using their position to pursue the collective common good. A masculine view is that collaboration undermines power thus creating weakness (Brunner, 2005). These "service" positions were deemed appropriate roles which enhanced the historical ascension of women into higher education administration. In this study, several women believed that part of their ascension into power was because of their commitment to the "greater good." This intersection between the vertical and horizontal culture may be blurred, but in deconstruction both the masculine and feminine binaries are needed for leadership; neither form is altogether absolute.

An element of deconstruction, includes a constant "self-revising, self-correcting, continual reaffirmation of itself, . . . , if it is to have a self, a 'yes' followed by a 'yes' and then again another 'yes'" (Caputo, 1997, p. 200). These women looked outside themselves and "say yes" to the needs of students and faculty; however, this attitude stays within the boundaries of the university's  goals. In this context, decision-making is not empowerment, but is still harnessed by the dean. The deans determine and shape what is knowledge and power, and "monopolize all relevant knowledge within an organization" (McKinlay & Starkey, 2000, p. 111). This is reminiscent of the Foucaultian view that 'truth' and 'knowledge' are socially constructed products of interests and power relations (Hines, 1988). Knowledge that appears to be hidden becomes powerful. There is power that resides in the leaders' actions yet also in the leader's discretion to conceal.

One dean defined power as the ability to make decisions that was measured through resource allocation. Another dean described power as being created through diversity. Power is created in multidimensional approaches. Although diversity and shared governance creates power, the deans understood that the institution owns the power, not the faculty or the dean. Like shared governance, delegation was described as a part of producing power in employees and in organizations.

The contrasting story of the dean who liked hoarding the important tasks illustrated the negation of the "gift" of power. Delegation is a leader's gift to employees; however, the paradox is that this gift is directed by the dean where the deans want to "give" power, but control it as well. There is a tension between the "gift" of freedom in decision-making and the deans' control of "mistakes." The deans recognized the dilemma in attempting to empower yet not giving authority, which then turns into control. The tension in this paradox is that employees cannot be empowered without the freedom of their own decision-making and vision. Empowerment is not the same as Derrida's "gift" because the people are only empowered if their goals coincide with administration's goals. This is then reframed by administration as "ownership."

The dean's role is to shape a joint organizational vision. As the leader, the dean persuades the faculty to own the institution's vision, but this creates an oppositional binary of resistance when faculty cannot align themselves to the institution. The "us" versus "them" power struggle is born and becomes amplified through managing via praise and reward. The deans' power resides in the convincing of others that they have ownership, but the deans acknowledged that their power comes from how others view them. A dean's power is her employees' gift to her, not something she owns. What distinguished the term power from authority is that authority is something sought and taken, not given. Leadership is a gift, and perhaps leadership does not exist in this context of higher education. On the other hand, the faculty's identity and prestige in academia rests on their alignment with the institution. A deconstructive element is that faculty cannot exist without the institution.

These women liked the term "influence" instead of "power," to reframe this management of people's behavior. The gift of leadership is only given when there is no control, and thus the deans are uncomfortable in using authority to move their agendas and struggled with this paradox. They were torn by the contradictions inherent in their roles as leaders in a masculine hierarchy, and their own personal values reflecting their feminine reproductive desires. This study revealed the amount of discomfort these women had with certain perspectives of power. These women disliked the masculine "power-over" control concept while emulating the "power-with" feminine characteristic. The deans liked the power inherent in their positions, but were uncomfortable with power-seeking behavior. These women wanted to generate power by empowering others and creating change via their reproductive roles. In Western culture, power is segmented into different forms but has been conceptualized as "dominance, control, authority, and influence over others and things" (Brunner, 2005, p. 126). But in these women's realities, power was something they struggled with internally.

In another context, the female-dominated deans seem to be "empire-building" as they attempted to hoard their power. As I looked at the text of the female-dominated deans, I perceived a pervasive need for power which translated into a pervasive sense of insecurity. My subjective reading of the text recognized a theme of degradation of their colleges' position in the academy which had been traditionally considered "powerless." The language of the deans from female-dominated colleges reflected nuances of control. In contrast, the need for power was much less prevalent with male-dominated deans whose language centered on service to students and faculty. All of the women interviewed were extremely bright and articulate; however, the negative aura of being from a female-dominated profession influenced those deans' speech and attitudes about their own professions.

Stereotypical absolutes are evident, but also revealed are the blurring of the gender lines. Power and gender are intimately related. Surprisingly, most of the deans did not speak of men in stereotypical or disparaging terms; although conversations about conflict with men provoked laughter. In spite of having grown up during the rebirth of feminism in the seventies, they did not have women role models. These deans had to learn leadership skills on their own and depended on male mentors as they rose in administration. While these women distinguished themselves from men, they also described themselves as men. By distinguishing the binary, these women became that which they stereotyped. Deans from female-dominated areas often described themselves as "male-like" who "wear it differently." The anger in the text was clear, with laughter interspersed within the stereotyping. These women share the perspectives of the first wave of feminism where women sought all the rights and privileges that men had, and women deserved equal rights because they wanted to be "just like" men.

As these women from female-dominated colleges described themselves as men, they were enacting a masculine conception of power, a role appropriate for their position, but not for their gender. Perhaps those women in female-dominated colleges face even higher expectations to manifest the "nurturing" role or face conflict with female colleagues. Those "gender-benders" may face more difficulties because their masculine traits may stand out in female-dominated colleges. As these deans become, "that of which they speak" (Sarup, 1988, p. 70), they rise in the patriarchal system and distance themselves from their female colleagues. In contrast, those women from male-dominated colleges never described themselves as "male-like," but frequently talked about creating a thick skin so they "don't feel so much anymore." Both groups of women place themselves in Adrienne Rich's "ontological basement" (Martin, 1985, p. 15) because the masculine ideology dominates their discourse, and they distance themselves from their feminine selves.

However, not all deans differentiated themselves by gender. Several were much more ambiguous about distinguishing definite characteristics between men and women emphasizing individual differences. In their language there was a lack of stereotyping, and identification of gender characteristics. These deans resonated to the emotional context of situations- a more feminine trait, although not identified as such. In this politic, there is not a simple hierarchical view of men oppressing women, but a view of systematic genderized discourses where identity dissolves into difference (St. Pierre & Pillow, 2000).

The text further unfolded a discourse of resistance through adaptability. A shifting understanding of resistance through adaptability was illustrated by the story of the former dean from a female-dominated college who would rely on her male dean colleagues to rescue her when she needed them. In this case, men obliged her needs, but did not grant power to her or to her traditionally "powerless" college. This was in contrast to the current dean who had appreciably improved the perceived power of the college. Although this dean acknowledged that "the guys" would discount her at times because of her status, there is no anger in the text. She gained "the guys" trust by working hard, showing assertiveness, and bringing data to present her position, therefore avoiding aggressive strategies and following a pattern of heteronormativity (Brunner, 2005). Humor was a tool of negotiation in the face of being discredited without forsaking self-respect.

In this case, the dean had a father who supported her education and her identity as well as a training ground of light-hearted competitiveness with her brother. This link with the past helped her manage her relationships with her male colleagues and lessen the bitterness in her negotiations with them. While a feminist may see her methods as acquiescing to the "guys," her methods are a form of resistance through adaptability. No matter the college, all participants had to learn to negotiate power with male colleagues. Unfolding resistance through adaptability helped these women negotiate power.

Although leadership strategies do not encourage leaders to "tower over" employees and tell them off, men can do this successfully in the hierarchy. Women who use aggressive strategies to negotiate power will suffer consequences because of unspoken social mores. Women who enact the masculine conceptions of power make others very uncomfortable around them (Brunner, 2005). One participant enacted a masculine conception of power disrupting gender constructions and suffered from feeling "raped" and was reorganized. She deconstructed this event by balancing her life through reflection, reframing the meaning of the event, and by holding onto her mission of service and survived. The dimensions of her life expanded and contracted as she sorted her thoughts during her catastrophic rearrangement. Although she suffered consequences from using aggressive strategies, unlike the previous example, she recovered through reframing and transformation. She too unfolded through resistance and adaptability.

## IMPLICATIONS

Deterritorialized identities, becoming masculine, becoming feminine, becoming powerful, becoming powerless, becoming stereotypes, and becoming difference: "that is what multiplicity is" (Deleuze & Guattari, 1987, p. 32). These things are not imitations because these deans are not playing "men" in a real way. The "becoming" multiplicities are real "even if that something other it becomes is not" (p. 32). For clarification, "becoming" lacks a subject distinct from itself. There is difficulty in drawing any conclusions or implications except to understand that within each individual there are multiple identities that are revealed in different societal contexts. There is nothing stable in this politics of poststructuralism and deconstruction.

However, the rich descriptions in this study illuminated the contextual interplay of these women specifically in their patriarchal, hierarchical realms. Their stories revealed that women leaders need to expect conflict and fragmentation, not only in their external lives, but in their internal lives as well. Their stories validated that women can be both reproducers of the species and producers of culture. There was evidence that creating a counterculture strengthens the oppositional binaries and erases individuality. The stories illustrated that "gender-bending" may result in "failed assimilation," as in Rahel's struggle with anti-Semitism, when women re-enact masculine characteristics of leadership. This research gave these women voice, but more importantly as other women identify with the stories of these participants, their reflections and writings will unfold new "becomings" for leadership.

Further research should include the silent voices of those that are employed by these women leaders. How do these administrative assistants view leadership? What are the voices of the "powerless" who can become powerful by their action or inaction? As Weiler (1988) suggested, the less powerful find creative and even powerful ways to resist, and individuals struggle to create their own meaning. Historically the research amply shows that men oppress women, but there is need for further study on how women oppress and limit themselves. "Gender-bending" was shown to not be an allowable social more, and more research is needed on how women perceive and act toward other women. How can women negotiate oppression from other women and themselves? What are the allowable "becomings" for women?

## EPILOGUE

In times of conflict, people reframe the text in order to survive. A mission of self-preservation does not protect us in times of crisis. Individuals get washed away and destroyed as their sense of self disappears. For myself, this writing has been a "becoming," and a "method of inquiry;" "writing is also a way of 'knowing'-a method of discovery and analysis" (Richardson, 2000, p. 923). As I reflected on these deans, my mind incessantly roamed to my sister who could not reframe her text, could not hold to a mission to direct her life, and whose life had been washed away. Looking through my sister's lens changed the texture and depth of my inquiry. A historical perspective reveals the tedious repetition of themes; women still have concerns of gender discrimination and sex role socialization. Women's attitudes themselves can be the most problematic. Looking at these deans' successes replenishes the soul; however, many women are still voiceless. We must never forget those who lost theirs.

*Appendix*

# Rhizo-Map: Lines of Becoming— Follow the Shades of Gray

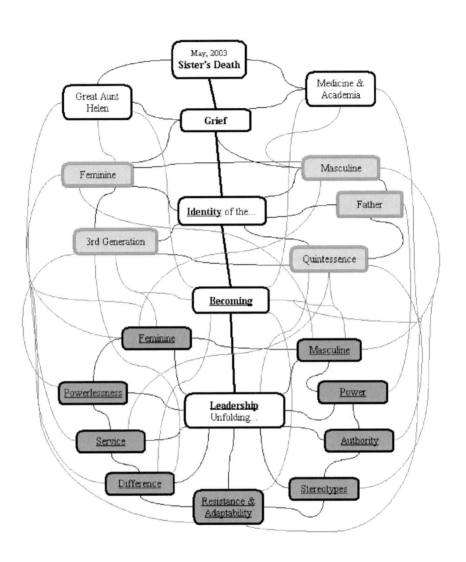

# References

Acker, J. (1990). Hierarchies, jobs, bodies: A theory of gendered organizations. *Gender and Society, 4*, 139-158.

Acker, S., & Feuerverger, G. (1996). Doing good and feeling bad. *Cambridge Journal of Education, 26*(3), 401-422.

Alvesson, M. & Skoldberg, K. (2001). *Reflexive methodology: New vistas for qualitative research.* Thousand Oaks, CA: Sage Publications.

Arendt, H. (1972). *Crises of the republic: Lying in politics, civil disobedience or violence thoughts on politics, and revolution.* New York: Harcourt, Brace, Jovanovich.

Association of American Medical Colleges. (2005). *Women in U.S. academic medicine: Statistics and medical school benchmarking.* Retrieved February 6, 2006, from http://www.aamc.org/members/wim/statistics/stats05/start.htm

Badiou, A. (1994). *Gilles Deleuze. The fold: Leibniz and the baroque.* In C. V. Boundas & D. Olkowski (eds.), *Gilles Deleuze and the theater of philosophy.* (pp. 51-69). New York: Routledge.

Behar, R. & Gordon, D. A. (1995). *Women writing culture.* Berkley, CA: University of California Press.

Belenky, M., Clinchy, B., Goldberger, N., & Tarule, J. (1986). *Women's ways of knowing: The development of self, voice and mind.* New York: Basic Books Inc.

Bellas, M. L. (1999). Emotional labor in academia: The case of professors. *Annals of the American Academy of Political and Social Science, 561,* 96-110.

Biklen, S., & Shakeshaft, C. (1985). The new scholarship on women. In S. Klein (Ed.), *Handbook for achieving sex equity through education* (pp. 44-52). Baltimore: Johns Hopkins University Press.

Blanchard, K., O'Connor, M., & Ballard, J. (1997). *Managing by values.* San Francisco: Berrett-Koehler Publishers.

Bolman, L. G. (2001). *Leading with soul: An uncommon journey of spirit.* San Francisco: Jossey-Bass.

Borg, W. R., Gall, J. P., & Gall, M. (1993). *Applying educational research: A practical guide.* White Plains, NY: Longman Publishing Group.

Bronstein, P., & Farnsworth, L. (1998). Gender differences in faculty experiences of interpersonal climate and processes for advancement. *Research in Higher Education,* 39, 557-585.

Brown, C. F. (2001). Patterns of leadership: The impact of female authority in four women's colleges, 1880-1910. In Nidiffer, J. & Bashaw, C. T. (Eds.), *Women administrators in higher education:Historical and contemporary perspectives.* (pp. 37-65) Albany, NY: SUNY Press.

Brunner, C. (2005). Women performing the superintendency: Problematizing the normative alignment of conceptions of power and constructions of gender. In J. Collard & C. Reynolds (Ed.), *Leadership, gender, & culture in education.* (pp.121-135) New York: Open University Press.

Brunner, C.C. and Schumaker, P. (1998). Power and gender in 'New View' public schools. *Policy Studies Journal,* 26(1): 30-45.

Caputo, J. D. (1997). *Deconstruction in a nutshell: A conversation with Jacques Derrida.* New York: Fordham University Press.

Carroll, L., Ellis, K. L., & McCrea, S. A. (1991). Benefits, risks, and reactions: The experiences of university professional women as advocates. *Initiatives, 54,* 1-7.

Carter-Scott, C. (1994). The differences between leadership and management. *Manage, 46*(2), 10-12.

Chandler, S. & Richardson, S. (2005). *100 ways to motivate others: How great leaders can produce insane results without driving people crazy.* Career Press.

Conley, F. K. (1998). *Walking out on the boys.* Farrar, Straus and Giroux: New York.

Costello, R. B. (Ed). (1994). *The American heritage dictionary* (3rd ed.). NY: Dell Publishing.

Court, M. (2005). Negotiating and reconstructing gendered leadership discourses. In J. Collard & C. Reynolds (Ed.), *Leadership, gender, & culture in education.* (pp. 3-17) New York: Open University Press.

Craib, I. (1992). *Modern social theory.* New York: St. Martin's Press.

Creswell, J. (1998). *Qualitative research and research design.* Thousand Oaks, CA: Sage Publications.

Crotty, M. (1998). *The foundations of social research: Meaning and perspective in the research process.* Thousand Oaks, CA: Sage Publications.

Crowley, J. N. (1994). *No equal in the world: An interpretation of the academic presidency.* Reno: University of Nevada Press.

Davidson, A. L. (1994). Border curricula and the construction of identity: Implications for multicultural theorists. *Qualitative Studies in Education, 7*(4), 335-349.

Deem, R. (Ed.). (1980). *Schooling for women's work.* London: Routledge & Kegan Paul.

Deleuze, G. (1988). *Foucault* (S. Hand, Trans.). Minneapolis, MN: University of Minnesota Press. (Original work published 1986)

Deleuze, G. (1993). *The fold: Leibniz and the baroque* (T. Conley, Trans.). Minneapolis, MN: University of Minneapolis Press. (Original work published 1988)

Deleuze, G., & Guattari, F. (1987). *A thousand plateaus: Capitalism and schizophrenia* (B. Massumi, Trans.). Minneapolis, MN: University of Minneapolis Press. (Original work published in 1980)

Derrida, J. (1981). *Positions.* Baltimore: Johns Hopkins University Press.

Dey, E. L., Korn, J. S., & Sax, L. F. (1996). Betrayed by the academy: The sexual harassment of women college faculty. *Journal of Higher Education, 67*(2), 149-173.

Etzioni, A. (1961). *A comparative analysis of complex organizations: On power, involvement, & their correlates.* NY: The Free Press.

Flax, J. (1990). Postmodernism and gender relations in feminist theory. In L. Nicholson (Ed.), *Feminism/postmodernism* (pp. 39-62). New York: Routledge.

Foucault, M. (2002). *The Archeology of Knowledge* (A. M. Sheridan Smith, Trans.). London; New York: Routledge. (Original work published 1972)

Foucault, M. (1988). *Technologies of the self* (L. H. Martin, H. Gutman, & P. H. Hutton Eds.). Amherst: University of Massachusetts Press.

Foucault, M. (1984). Truth and power. In P. Rabinow (Ed.), *Foucault reader.* (pp. 51-75). New York: Pantheon Books.

Foucault, M. (1980). *Power/Knowledge: Selected interviews & other writings 1972-1977* (C. Gordon, L. Marshall, J. Mepham, & K. Soper, Trans.). In C. Gordon (Ed.). New York: Pantheon Books.

Frank, E., brogan, D. and Schiffman, M. (1998). Prevalence and correlates of harassment among US women physicians. *Archives of Internal Medicine, 158, 352-8.*

Freire, P. (1998). *Pedagogy of Freedom.* Lanham, MD: Rowman & Littlefield Publishers.

French, J. R., & Raven, B. (1959). Bases of social power. In C. Dorwin (Ed.), *Studies    In social power* (pp. 150-167). Ann Arbor: University of Michigan Press.

Giroux, H. A. (2001). Vocationalizing higher education: Schooling and the politics of corporate culture. In Giroux, H. A. & Myrsiades, K. (Eds.), *Beyond the corporate university* (pp.29-44). Lanham, MD: Rowman & Littlefield Publishers.

Gordon, B. M. (2001). Knowledge construction, competing critical theories, and education. In J. A. Banks & C. A. McGee-Banks (Eds.), *Handbook of Research of Multicultural Education* (pp. 184-216). San Francisco, CA: Jossey-Bass.

Greenleaf, R. K. (1979). *Teacher as servant.* New York: Paulist Press.

Grogan, M. (2003). Laying the groundwork for a reconception of the superintendency from feminist postmodern perspectives. In M. D. Young & L. Skrla (Eds.), *Reconsidering feminist research in educational leadership* (pp. 9-34). Albany, NY: SUNY Press.

Guberman, R. (Ed.). (1996). *Julia Kristeva interviews.* New York: Columbia University Press.

Gubrium, J. & Holstein, J. (2003). *Poststructural interviewing.* Thousand Oaks, CA: Sage Publications Inc.

Habermas, J. (1986). *Legitimation crisis.* Boston: Beacon Press.

Hargreaves, A. (1994). *Changing teachers, changing times.* New York: Teachers College Press.

Harstock, N. (1987). Foucault on power: a theory for women? In L. Nicholson (ed.), *Feminism/Postmodernism* (pp. 157-175). London: Routledge.

Heifetz, R. A., & Linsky, M. (2002). *Leadership on the line: Staying alive through the dangers of leading.* Boston: Harvard Business School Press.

Hershey, P., Blanchard, K., & Johnson, D. E. (2001). *Management of organizational behavior: Leading human resources.* Upper Saddle River, N.J.: Prentice Hall.

Hinze, S. W. (2004). 'Am I being oversensitive?' Women's experience of sexual harassment during medical training. *Health: An Interdisciplinary Journal for the Social Study of Health, Illness, and Medicine, 8*(1), 101-127.

Holmes, L. (1939). *A history of the position of dean of women in a selected group of
co-educational colleges and universities in the United States.* New York: Teachers
College, Columbia University, Bureau of Publications.

Isaac, J. (1993). Beyond the three faces of power: a realist critique, In T. Wartenberg
(ed.). *Rethinking Power.* Albany, NY: SUNY Press.

Kanter, R. M. (1977). *Men and women of the corporation.* New York: Basic Books.

Kanter, R. M. (1979). Power, leadership, and participatory management. *Theory into
Practice, 20*(4) pp 219-224.

Karnes, F. A., Chauvin, J. C. (2005). *Leadership development program: Leadership
skills inventory and leadership development program manual* (2nd ed.). Scottsdale,
AZ: Great Potential Publishing.

Kelly, G., & Nihlen, A. (1982). Schooling and the reproduction of patriarchy: Unequal
workloads, unequal rewards. In M. Apple (Ed.), *Cultural and economic reproduction in education.* London: Routledge and Kegan Paul.

Kirkpatrick, J. J. (1974). *Political woman.* New York: Basic Books.

Kristeva, J. (1995). *New maladies of the soul* (R. Guberman, Trans.). New York: Columbia University Press.

Kristeva, J. (2001). *Hannah Arendt* ( R. Guberman, Trans.). New York: Columbia
University Press.

Lakoff, G. & Johnson, M. (1980). *Metaphors we live by.* Chicago: University of Chicago Press.

Lather, P. (1993). Fertile obsession: Validity after poststructuralism. *Sociological
Quarterly, 34,* 673-693.

Lather, P. (1996, April). *Methodology as subversive repetition: Practices toward a
feminist double science.* Paper presented at the annual meeting of the American
Educational Research Association, New York City.

Lewis, C. S. (1981). *A grief observed.* New York: Bantam Books.

Lincoln, Y. S. (1986). The ladder and the leap. *Educational Horizons, 64,* 113-116.

Lincoln, Y. S. & Guba, E. G. (2000). Paradigmatic controversies, contradictions, and
emerging confluences. In Denzin, N. & Lincoln, Y. (Eds.). *Handbook of qualitative
research.* (pp.163-188). Thousand Oaks, CA: Sage Publications.

Luke, C. (2001). *Globalization and women in academia: North/West-South/East.*
Mahwah, NJ: Lawrence Erlbaum Associates, Inc.

Lyotard, J. (1984). *The postmodern condition: A report on knowledge* (G. Benning-
ton & B. Massumi, Trans.). Minneapolis: University of Minnesota Press. (Original
work published 1979)

Macey, D. (2000). *The penguin dictionary of critical theory.* London: Penguin
Books.

Marshall, M. R. & Jones, C. H. (1990). Childbearing sequence and the career development of women administrators in higher education. *Journal of College Student
Development, 31,* 531-537.

Martin, J. R. (1985). *Reclaiming a conversation: The ideal of the educated woman.*
New Haven, CT: Yale University Press.

Martin, S., Arnold, R. and Parker, R. (1988). Gender and medical socialization. *Journal of Health and Social Behavior, 29*, 333-43.

McAfee, N. (2004). *Kristeva.* New York: Routledge.

McKinlay, A. & Starkey, K. (ed.) (2000). *Foucault, Management and Organization Theory.* London: Sage Publications.

Merrill, M. (2004). *Dare to lead-unconventional sense and unconventional wisdom from 50 top CEOs.* Franklin Lakes, NJ: Career Press.

Mills, S. (2004). *Discourse.* London: Routledge.

Miller, J. B. (1993). Women and power. In T. Wartenberg (ed.). *Rethinking power.* Albany, NY: SUNY Press.

Mishler, E. G. (1986). *Research interviewing: Context and narrative.* Cambridge, MA: Harvard University Press.

Nidiffer, J. (2000). *Pioneering deans of women: More than wise and pious matrons.* New York: Teachers College Press.

Nidiffer, J. & Bashaw, C. T. (2001). *Women administrators in higher education: Historical and contemporary perspectives.* Albany, NY: SUNY Press

O'brien, S. (1987). *Willa Cather.* New York: Oxford University Press.

OECD. 1987. *Universities under Scrutiny.* William Taylor. Paris: OECD.

Olesen, V. L. (2000). Feminisms and qualitative research at and into the millennium. In Denzin, N. & Lincoln, Y. (Eds.). *Handbook of qualitative research.* (pp.215-256). Thousand Oaks, CA: Sage Publications.

Palmer, D. D. (1998). *Structuralism and poststructuralism for beginners.* New York: Writers and Readers Publishing Inc.

Park, S. M. (1996). Research, teaching, and service: Why shouldn't women's work count? *Journal of Higher Education. 67*(1) January/February p.47-83.

Passow, A. H. (1988). Styles of leadership training and some more thoughts. *The Gifted Child Today. (11)*6, 34-38.

Perino, S., & Perino, J. (1988). What characteristics need to be developed in students for them to be considered leaders? *Gifted Child Today, 11*(6), 23.

Peters, M. A. (2001) *Postructuralism,Marxism, and neoliberalism: Between theory and Politics.* Lanham, MD: Rowman & Littlefield Publishers.

Porter, J. (1989). Leadership and ownership within student affairs. *NASPA Journal, (27)* 1, 11-17.

Richardson, L. (1997). *Fields of play: Constructing an academic life.* New Brunswick, NJ: Rutgers University Press.

Richardson, L. (2000). Writing: A method of inquiry. In N. Denzin, & Y. Lincoln (Eds.), *Handbook of qualitative research* (pp. 923-948). Thousand Oaks, CA: Sage Publications.

Sarup, M. (1988). *An introductory guide to post-structuralism and postmodernism.* New York: Harvester Wheatsheaf.

Saussure, F. (1983). *Course in general linguistics* (R. Harris, Trans.). London: Duckworth. (Original work published 1949)

Scheurich, J. J. (1995). A postmodernist critique of research interviewing. *Qualitative Studies in Education, 8*(3), 239-252.

Schwandt, T. (2001). *Dictionary of qualitative research.* Thousand Oaks, CA: Sage Publications, Inc.

Scott, J. (1986). Gender: A useful category of historical analysis, *American Historical Review, 91,* 1053-1075.

Sergiovanni, T. J. (1990). *Value-added leadership: How to get extraordinary performance in schools.* San Diego, CA: Harcourt, Brace Jovanovich.

Shultz, E. L., & Easter, L. M. (1997). A study of professional aspirations and perceived obstacles: A case for administrative change. (Report No. SP-037-820). Kutztown, PA: Kutztown, University. (ERIC Document Reproduction Service No. ED417174)

Silverman, D. (Eds.). (1998). *Qualitative research: Theory, method, and practice.* Thousand Oaks, CA: Sage Publications, Inc.

Smart, J. C. (1991). Gender equity in academic rank and salary. *The Review of Higher Education, 14*(4), 551-526.

Solomon, B.M. (1985). *In the company of educated women.* New Haven and London: Yale University Press.

St. Pierre, E. A. (1997). Methodology in the fold and the irruption of transgressive data. *Qualitative Studies in Education, 10*(2), 175 189.

St. Pierre, E. A. (2005, January). *Writing as a method of nomadic inquiry.* Paper presented at the annual conference on Interdisciplinary Qualitative Studies, Athens, GA.

St. Pierre, E. A. & Pillow, W. S. (Eds.). (2000). *Working the ruins: Feminist poststructural theory and methods in education.* New York: Routledge.

Toutkoushian, R. K. (1999). The status of academic women in the 1990s: No longer outsiders, but not yet equals. *The Quarterly Review of Economics and Finance, 39,* 679-698.

Treichler, P. A. (1985). Alma mater's sorority: Women and the University of Illinois, 1890-1925. In P. A. Treichler, C. Kramarae, & B. Stafford (Eds.), *For alma mater: Theory and practice in feminist scholarship* (pp. 24). Urbana: University of Illinois Press.

Urlich, L. T. (1976). Vertuous women found: New England ministerial literature, 1668-1735. *American Quarterly, 28*(1), 20-40.

Wartenberg, T. E. (1990). *The forms of power: From domination to transformation.* Philadelphia: Temple University Press.

Weedon, C. (1997). *Feminist practice and poststructuralist theory.* (2nd ed.). New York: Basil Blackwell.

Weiler, K. (1988). *Women teaching for change: gender, class & power.* New York: Bergin & Garvey.

Weiler, K. (2003). Feminist analyses of gender and schooling. In A. Darder, M. Baltodano & R. D. Torres (Eds.), *The Critical Pedagogy Reader* (pp. 269-295). New York: Routledgefalmer.

Weissberg. L. (Ed.). (1997). *Rahel Varnhagen: The life of a Jewess* (R. & C. Winston, Trans.). Baltimore: Johns Hopkins University Press.

Wenniger, M. D., & Conroy, M. H. (Eds.). (2001). *Gender equity or bust!: On the road to campus leadership with women in higher education.* San Francisco: Jossey-Bass.

Woods, T. (1999). *Beginning Postmodernism.* Manchester, UK: Manchester University Press.

# Index

adaptability (accommodation), 14, 21-22, 72, 75, 81
Arendt, Hannah, 18, 24-25
authority, 16-17, 21-22, 32-33, 39, 44, 53, 58-60, 78-79

binary, 1-3, 8, 12, 27-28, 34-36, 43, 46, 52, 54, 58, 65, 69, 72, 76, 78-80, 82

"Chilly climate," 14, 69
collaboration, 7, 11, 19, 49-52, 73-75, 78
control, 5, 17, 34, 39, 49, 52-53, 55, 57-60, 64, 73, 78-79

deans of women, 9-12, 38, 68
deconstruction, 3, 8, 16, 22, 26-29, 32, 35, 46, 50, 52, 57, 62, 65, 67, 76, 78-79, 81-82
Deleuze, Gilles, 3, 27-28, 34-36, 46, 62, 76-77, 82
Derrida, Jacques, 4, 22, 27-29, 57, 59, 79
discourse, 2-8, 16-19, 26-27, 37, 53, 71-72
discursive formation, 4, 27, 47, 59

empowerment, 17, 19, 44, 52, 59, 78-79

fathers, role of, 5, 38-39, 68, 70, 75-76, 81
feminism: historical, 1, 3, 20-21, 23-24, 53; feminist poststructuralism, 3, 7, 9, 22, 24, 26, 29, 32-33; social feminism, 21-22. *See also* Kristeva, Julia
"fold," the, 28, 33-34, 36-37, 40-46, 49, 52, 62-63, 65, 72, 75-77, 81-82
Foucault, 4-6, 12, 22, 27, 29, 33, 47, 52-54, 56, 59, 61, 71, 78

"gender-bending," 14, 29, 63, 68-70, 80-82
gender roles, 5, 12-13, 18, 49-50, 68-69, 72-73
gendered organization, 12, 46
gift, 52, 55, 57, 59, 78-79
Guattari, Félix, 3, 27-28, 34-36, 46, 76-77, 82

hierarchy, 4, 16, 20, 27, 36, 44, 48-49, 52, 54, 62, 65, 73, 76, 78-79, 81

knowledge, 2-5, 7, 26-27, 30, 33, 35, 47, 52-57, 72, 78
Kristeva, Julia, 4, 9, 22-25, 27, 35, 41, 56

# About the Author

**Carol A. Isaac** was born in Central Kansas and graduated with a music education degree from the University of Kansas. Being brought up in a medical family, she transitioned into teaching science and eventually returned to school where in 1988 she earned a Bachelors of Health Science in Physical Therapy from the University of Florida. As a physical therapist, Carol pursued clinical education, developing students into professionals. Eventually, she was promoted into hospital administration, where she learned firsthand the alluring and arduous challenges of leadership. While a departmental manager, Carol began her masters and then finished a Ph.D. in Educational Administration at the University of Florida. That course of study began her fascination with women's history and leadership. During that period, Carol learned that her grandmother had initiated a student affairs program where she found jobs for college students during the Depression and World War II. Carol also learned that her great aunt was the first women dean at a small Mennonite college in the 1920's. This great aunt had grown up with her two aunts who were the first women doctors in Kansas during the late nineteenth and early twentieth centuries. Carol's academic interests are a continuation of her predecessors' legacy.